P9-DIB-457

GARDENING
in CONTAINERS

fine
Gardening Design Guides™

GARDENING
in CONTAINERS

Creative Ideas *from* America's Best Gardeners

The Taunton Press

q 635.986
Gardening
Rennell

Special thanks to the editors, art directors, copy editors, and other staff members of Fine Gardening *who contributed to the development of the articles in this book.*

Other books in the series include: *Accent Your Garden, Creating Beds and Borders, Designing with Plants, Exploring Garden Style,* and *Landscaping Your Home.*

Text © 2002 by The Taunton Press, Inc.
All rights reserved.

The Taunton Press
Inspiration for hands-on living™

The Taunton Press, Inc., 63 South Main Street, PO Box 5506, Newtown, CT 06470-5506
e-mail: tp@taunton.com

Distributed by Publishers Group West

Fine Gardening Design Guides™ is a trademark of The Taunton Press. Inc., registered in the U.S. Patent and Trademark Office.

COVER AND INTERIOR DESIGNER: Lori Wendin

LAYOUT ARTIST: Lori Wendin

FRONT COVER PHOTOGRAPHER: © Randy O'Rourke

BACK COVER PHOTOGRAPHERS: Delilah Smittle, © The Taunton Press, Inc. (large); Steve Silk, © The Taunton Press, Inc. (top left); © Lee Anne White (top right); © Steve Buchanan (bottom center)

LIBRARY OF CONGRESS CATALOGING-IN-PUBLICATION DATA
Gardening in containers : creative ideas from America's best gardeners.
     p. cm.—(Fine gardening design guides)
  ISBN 1-56158-557-2
    1. Container gardening.   I. Taunton Press.   II. Series.
SB418 .G377 2002
   635.9'86—dc21   2001042524

4736920

Printed in the United States of America
10 9 8 7 6 5 4 3 2 1

Gardening in containers is highly seductive, because the gardener is in control, more than is possible in any other kind of gardening."

– Allen Lacy
In a Green Shade

Contents

Introduction

There is a tendency to think of container plantings only as an accent for the patio, front door, or window, but containers offer gardeners so much more. Container gardens allow us to experiment with different plant combinations without planting a flower bed, or create a landscape where it would otherwise be impossible—say on the 37th floor of a New York high rise. And if we'd rather have those plants next to these plants, well, all we have to do is heft a pot or two, and in a minute we've rearranged the garden.

Within the landscape, potted plants fill empty spaces and serve as focal points. They're ideal for marking the entrance to a garden room or highlighting a flight of stairs. They also allow us the indulgence of adding tropical plants to temperate gardens for a few months before they must go indoors. Just about anything will grow in pots, so we can place them in either sunny or shady locations.

In *Gardening in Containers,* some of America's best gardeners share their tips for growing plants in containers. They'll demonstrate how to design great plant combinations; choose and care for pots; and grow plants, such as bulbs, succulents, roses, and even trees, in containers. They'll also help you choose the best potting soil, install a drip irrigation system for pots, and keep your container garden looking good all season long. For years, they've been sharing their insights in *Fine Gardening* magazine. Now you have their work in a single book that will guide and inspire you to create your own container garden.

CONTAINERS
IN THE GARDEN

1

ANYONE CAN GARDEN IN CONTAINERS—whether they live on a large plot of land, hang their hat in a Manhattan apartment building, or have little more than a sunny windowsill. Container plantings can accent an existing garden, dress up a doorway, or be used to create an entire garden on a deck or patio. They can fill bare spots in the sunny garden with a burst of color, or lighten a shady garden with a touch of white flowers or variegated foliage.

The great thing about container gardening is its versatility. You can create a miniature garden in a single pot with several plants, or combine several pots of individual plants to create a compact garden. You can place pots on the ground, atop tables, below a window, or hanging from a porch or tree limb. And if you love the sight and sound of water, you can even create a container water garden in a trough, barrel, or small pot.

Pots
Have a
Place
in the Garden

GORDON HAYWARD

is a garden designer, lecturer, and writer in Putney, Vermont. He and his wife have led garden tours in England and Ireland.

(LEFT) Pots need not be filled with plants to make a strong impression in the landscape.

(INSET) Group potted plants directly in the garden.

THE ENTRANCE TO OUR GARDEN here in southern Vermont was satisfying enough—a break in a yew hedge; a young weeping larch (*Larix decidua* 'Pendula') to the left; a few stone steps surrounded by *Sedum acre* and *Paxistima canbyi*; and a big, broad planting of 'Cherry Cheeks' daylilies on both sides. But still, it lacked pizzazz. There was little or no open soil for new plants, but there was room on the stone steps for planted containers. So we put lots of them on either side of the steps to welcome visitors into our garden.

COLOR THROUGHOUT THE SEASON

In just one 22-inch-diameter terra-cotta pot there in our entrance garden, we created a wonderful progression of color from April until the end of October: brilliant red tulips for almost a month, which we then uprooted and replaced in mid-May with the dark red *Fuchsia*

The corner of a patio is a perfect spot for a cluster of pots where they can serve as a visual anchor.

Planted containers perform well in the center of a small garden. We placed a weeping pea shrub (*Caragana arborescens* 'Pendula') in a pot, underplanted it with cascading, *Bacopa caroliniana,* and set it at the center of our four-quadrant herb garden. I've also used jardinieres and fine antique pots at the center of small gardens.

POTS BRIGHTEN SHADY AREAS

Containers add color to parts of the garden that lack interest during certain times of the year. We've hung pots of cascading pink geraniums (*Pelargonium peltatum* 'Balcon') just above blue false indigo (*Baptisia australis*) to create a pleasing color combination. We planted *Hosta* 'Shade Fanfare' with its yellow variegation along with a lovely yellow-flowering *Kirengeshoma palmata* to lighten an otherwise shady area.

We've planted 5- to 7-foot-high yellow-flowering angels' trumpets (*Brugmansia arborea*) in large, lightweight, terra-cotta—colored plastic pots. Then to camouflage the plastic, we underplanted the angels' trumpets with draping *Helichrysum petiolare* 'Variegatum', whose leaves have a chartreuse and light green variegation. Last summer, one of these angels' trumpets had more than eighty 10-inch-long, fragrant trumpets in bloom at once. Each September, we move this tropical plant to a greenhouse for over-wintering.

'Gartenmeister Bonstedt' underplanted with *Scaevola* 'Blue Wonder' and the chartreuse-leaved *Helichrysum petiolare* 'Limelight', followed in September by bronze and dark red chrysanthemums. Not bad for less than 3 square feet of garden space.

I have found that there are any number of uses for pots in the garden. Place a container planted with bright red, clear white, and vibrant yellow flowers at the end of a long, sunny path, and you can see it from quite a distance. Such a brightly colored combination draws people along a path, becoming a destination. A second pot might be placed further along the path to attract visitors deeper into your garden.

I've always found that paths provide clues for placing pots. And an entrance to a new garden is always a good spot for pots—heightening the awareness that you're entering a new space. Last year, we planted three 5-foot, gray-leaved cardoons (*Cynara cardunculus*) in a 24-inch pot next to some yews at the entrance to a garden; the gray leaves looked wonderful against the dark green hedge.

USE POTS AS DESIGN ELEMENTS

We've also placed empty glazed or terra-cotta containers at the end of a path or at the apex of a curve in a path, signaling that this is the way to wander through our garden. Once, we set an empty, 40-inch-high Columbian pot at the beginning of a pathway and a smaller, similarly shaped, 32-inch pot in a curve further along the same pathway, but in view of the first pot. This creates the illusion that the garden is larger than it really is.

We've also placed large pots at the end of the *Viburnum prunifolium* hedges at the outer edges of our herb garden, and planted them with blue lacecap hydrangeas (*Hydrangea macrophylla*). One year we underplanted them with brick-red nasturtium (*Tropaeolum majus* 'Empress of India'); another year we used perennial dusty miller (*Artemisia stelleriana* 'Silver Brocade').

Planted pots can also be placed at the base of pergola or arbor uprights, on the sides of steps or stairs, in the corners of patios, or at the entrance to terraces. Placed on casters, planters can be used in a variety of ways. For instance, several pots could define a small breakfast area at one end of a large terrace, then later be rolled to another spot when a party calls for a bigger space.

The containers themselves can add interest to a garden. We have a concrete urn displaying an oak-leaf pattern that is so handsome we simply leave it unplanted in our dining area. When guests are coming for dinner, we fill the urn with water and float flowers in it. I've also seen antique, unplanted Etruscanlike urns and Greek-style amphora add a note of romance to a garden. They can be set into perennial gardens, or at the entrance to sitting areas.

Stylish containers, either thoughtfully planted or left to shine on their own, can add an exciting, new dimension to your garden.

As focal points, pots draw your attention from one area of the garden to another.

A Movable Garden

SYDNEY EDDISON

is a long-time contributor to *Fine Gardening*. She has written numerous gardening books, including *The Self-Taught Gardener*.

(LEFT) The best thing about a potted garden is that everything is portable, especially when pots are light-weight, like the foam one the author is carry-ing here.

(INSET) Beautiful pots can also serve as focal points. This striking blue ceramic bowl is brimming with New Zealand flax, salvia, a deep-red geranium, coleus, and a licorice plant.

IN RECENT SUMMERS, the north-facing terrace that wraps around the back of our old farmhouse has looked like an in-ground garden. But the plants there are all in containers. This movable, different-every-year garden gives me enormous pleasure for minimum labor. It is a place where I try risky color schemes and experiment with unusual annuals and ten-der perennials. It is a place where I practice garden design without having to dig. In short, it's a place where I can have my cake and eat it, too.

TERRACE BECOMES A GARDEN

While I have always enjoyed assembling plant combina-tions in containers, making the whole terrace into a gar-den with structure and focal points is a relatively new venture. It all began when we gave up trying to make the

The creative arrangement of potted plants creates a garden-within-a-garden, while a low brick wall separates the terrace from the lawn.

12-foot-wide, 33-foot-long slab of cement we inherited with the house into an outdoor living space.

Years ago, we tried to relieve the ugliness of the cement by adding a low brick wall. While the soft, warm color of the old bricks took the curse off the cement, the enclosed space was even less congenial. The terrace was just too narrow for a comfortable grouping of garden furniture. It was also too hot in the summer. From June to August, it bakes in the sun for eight hours a day.

Ironically, everything that was wrong from a human perspective proved right for potted plants. My geraniums loved the heat and the sun. The cucumbers in containers grew like weeds, their trailing vines cascading down the sides of the half whiskey barrels and creeping along the paved surface. Soon, the low walls were given over to pots of rosemary, barrels of patio tomatoes, and window boxes of petunias and nasturtiums.

GROUPING POTS GIVES SHAPE TO THE SPACE

The terrace serves as an entrance into the main garden from the sliding glass doors in the kitchen. Opposite these doors, a comparable opening in the low brick wall leads onto the lawn, providing a view down the long axis of the garden. An axis is just an imaginary straight line, a spine along which elements of a garden can be arranged. I understood this concept in the larger landscape, and found that an axial arrangement on the terrace proved valuable, too.

To make the boxcar-shaped terrace more interesting, it needed to be divided. It made sense to imagine a linear axis running from the entrance at the narrow end to the middle of the wall at the far end. One year, I used an Australian rosemary (*Westringia fruticosa*, also known as *W. rosmariniformis*) standard set on the wall for a focal point. The wall gave the potted plant added height and importance.

From the start, I had been putting pots of geraniums (*Pelargonium* spp.) on either side of the wide opening in the low brick wall between the terrace and the garden. But I soon realized that to hold their own with the view, the containers themselves needed to be bigger. So I bought two pots 20 inches high and 24 inches across. At first, I clung to my early planting scheme of red geraniums surrounding tall, spiky *Dracaena marginata*, with *Vinca major* draped over the edges of the containers. Later, I made more adventurous choices, such as cannas (*Canna* cvs.), coleus (*Solenostemon scutellarioides* cvs.), and bronze fennel (*Foeniculum vulgare* 'Purpureum').

There are two other openings in the brick wall. One at the narrow end links the terrace to the breezeway. This is the approach to the garden that visitors use. A second opening at the far end of the terrace provides access to the dog run. Both entrances are vital. The first needed emphasis to announce its function and appear welcoming; the second needed to be disguised.

DISGUISE AN EYESORE WITH A VINE-LADEN ARBOR

Emphasizing the visitor's entrance with larger pots and groupings of smaller pots was relatively easy. The dog run, however, required a different technique. Instead of drawing attention to the opening, I wanted to hide it. So I built an arbor out of maple saplings and grew annual vines on it. The gate to the run was still accessible through a swinging curtain of tendrils, leaves, and flowers, but it didn't advertise itself. To obscure an eyesore, vines have to be vigorous and leafy. My favorites for this purpose are scarlet runner

To make the boxcar shape of the terrace more appealing, the author created a linear axis that runs the length of the space. Potted plants are lavishly grouped on both sides and a graceful table anchors the far end.

A wrought iron table and chair are a focal point when you enter the garden

Plants and structures can be moved until just the right place is found.

A wooden arch adds a formal element and highlights the terrace's entry.

A fountain marks a terrace corner defining the garden's border.

bean (*Phaseolus coccineus*), moonflower vine (*Ipomoea alba*), and 'Heavenly Blue' morning glories (*Ipomoea tricolor* 'Heavenly Blue').

As more plants and pots accumulated on the terrace, I began massing them at the entrance and in groups on either side of the imaginary axis. By the end of the season, only a path from one end of the terrace to the other remained between nasturtiums (*Tropaeolum majus*) and sweet potato vines (*Ipomoea batatas*). What started out as a miscellaneous collection of potted plants has evolved into a real garden.

Then I found a cedar arch that fit exactly into the narrow opening in the brick wall where visitors enter. Finally, the terrace garden was complete. It was amazing what this simple structure accomplished. Although the lattice sides were light and open, they hid part of the terrace so that visitors didn't know quite what to expect. What had been an exposed, open space, now seemed a private, almost secret enclosure. Growing a dainty but lusty clematis (*Clematis tangutica*) in pots on either side of the arch provided the finishing touch.

ADD FOCAL POINTS TO STRENGTHEN THE DESIGN

The arch also introduced a slightly formal element and seemed to call for a different treatment of the space it framed. I was reminded of a design principle I learned from my gardening friend Peter Wooster. He calls it "addressing the corners."

The rectilinear beds in Peter's garden explode with myriad textures, shapes, colors, heights, and plant forms, but the excess is subtly contained. Each bed is given structure by emphatic plants in the corners and centers. These emphatic plants may be evergreens or deciduous shrubs, and they serve as brackets, defining the corners and holding the gardens within their embrace.

"Making a garden on your terrace can either be a dress rehearsal for in-ground gardening or an end in itself."

To draw attention to the corners of the terrace, I needed something man-made to reinforce the sense of formality and enclosure. A graceful 6-foot trellis made of twisted grapevines did the trick in one corner, while a fountain did the same in the other.

The fountain, my pride and joy, is the joint effort of our friends Elizabeth McDonnell, a ceramic artist, and Trevor Youngberg, a potter. A little jet of water shoots upward from the beautiful ceramic ball Elizabeth made

Maintaining a Potted Garden

While a potted garden is physically undemanding, it does require vigilance. Since the garden is small and the plants are viewed at close range, grooming is critical. Regular removal of dead flowers from annuals not only makes them look better, it also keeps them flowering. Don't hesitate to cut back foliage plants whose branches get too long and ungainly. Take scissors or clippers and cut the stems back to a pair of leaves.

Watering is the trickiest chore because it is weather dependent. The hotter the temperature, the more often you have to water. The rate of evaporation also depends on the pot. A big container retains moisture longer than a small one. Also, plastic pots hold moisture longer than porous clay and wooden containers.

I water my pots almost every day from June to September. As the weather gets cooler and the days shorter, I water less often. Soak the soil so water runs out of the drainage holes. Allow the plants to use up that water before you add more.

Watering and fertilizing can be done together. Every week or two during the height of the season, I dissolve a balanced fertilizer in the watering can and apply it to all the potted plants. I fertilize less frequently from September on.

As the gardening season winds down, I move some plants indoors for the winter, like the Australian rosemary, and I take cuttings of others like my beloved *Brugmansia*. Eventually, Jack Frost gets the rest. Plant remains go to the compost pile and I use the spent soil to fill holes in the lawn. I store my pots in a shed for the winter, except for the large wood and plastic planters, which can stand the rigors of the season. I remove half of the soil from these, and replenish it in the spring.

Focal points can be small and portable in a terrace garden. This fountain was moved from spot to spot until a permanent home was found for the summer.

to 18 inches across. Last year, I planted it with red geraniums, glowing spikes of salmon-pink and olive-green New Zealand flax (*Phormium tenax*), a peach-colored salvia (*Salvia splendens* 'Carabiniere Orange'), and a coleus with pink patterns on the cocoa-brown leaves.

EXPERIMENT WITH COLOR

I love color. Until I had a garden, I had to make do with paints—watercolors and oils—but nothing has given me as much pleasure as arranging and rearranging leaf and flower colors. Putting together a cohesive color scheme in the garden requires time and considerable horticultural expertise. But putting colors together in containers is easy.

You can afford to try wild associations, like magenta petunias (*Petunia* cvs.) with Mexican flame vine (*Senecio confusus*). I love experimenting with jarring contrasts on the one hand and graduated color harmonies on the other. A successful combination in pots may give you ideas for your in-ground garden. An unsuccessful scheme is easily remedied: Move the pots or pull out the offending plant.

Making a garden on your terrace can be a dress rehearsal for in-ground gardening or an end in itself. For the past three summers, I have tried different color schemes and experimented with new plants. What is fun is the flexibility and freedom it gives me.

Every summer, layers of planting rise from the paving on my terrace garden. The trailing plants grow into each other and form ground covers, while the taller, bushier plants, like geraniums, coleus, and New Guinea impatiens fill the midborder positions. The cannas seem to reach as tall as the soaring stands of Joe Pye weed (*Eupatorium fistulosum* 'Gateway') in the perennial border.

I even have trees in my garden-within-a-garden. The angels' trumpets (*Brugmansia*

and subsides into Trevor's shallow bowl, supported on a matching pedestal.

The fountain's location was much debated. I carried it from corner to corner trying it in different positions. I tried it in the middle of a long stretch of wall on one side of the main opening, but felt it was wasted there. The entrance corner won out. And that's just one advantage of a terrace garden: structural features and focal points can be small and portable, like the fountain. They can be moved around until they are in the right place.

At the far end of the terrace, opposite and centered on the arch, is a wrought iron table. Secondhand and rather worse for wear, the table is still graceful and serves as a stand for my best pot—a blue ceramic bowl 9 inches deep that rises from an 11-inch base and flares

'Charles Grimaldi'), grown each year from cuttings, shoot up to 6 feet during the season, and by August, they shade the potted plants at their feet. The effect of the total garden surprises and delights me.

Imagine a garden where you can divide the space in a different way every year. By arranging pots in groups, curves, or straight lines, you can make hedges and paths. You can create beds by planting trailing plants as ground covers in the same pots with large plants, and by staggering the sizes of your pots.

Think of your potted garden like an in-ground border. You want edging plants and background plants; different heights and sizes; an interesting horizon with ups and downs; and contrasts in shapes of flowers and foliage. You can tinker with your potted border all summer. If a plant gets too big, move it. Instead of a backbreaking hour, it will take you a few minutes.

Big pots have to remain in place once planted, but smaller pots can be shuffled around to your heart's content. If you decide in mid-summer that you want something different, add or subtract a few containers.

Single plants in pots can be popped in and out of arrangements, and recombined in different ways. Large containers using several different kinds of plants are more of a challenge, but that's part of the fun. As a rule, even a large container, such as a half whiskey barrel, looks better when the variety of plants is limited to three or four kinds.

But rules are made to be broken. The real joy of making a garden with potted plants is that you actually *can* have it all. You can take risks and get away with it. You can go overboard without going bankrupt. You can have a beautiful garden without killing yourself with work. It's a win-win situation.

There are even trees grown in containers. Angels' trumpets shoot up to 6 feet and shade other pots on the terrace.

JOSEPH TOMOCIK

is the water-garden curator at the Denver Botanic Gardens, where his gardens include more than 80 small container water gardens.

A Tiny Water Garden

Exciting compositions spring from unusual combinations. The author used tall, spiky cattail (*Typha laxmannii*), broad-leaved cranberry taro (*Colocasia rubra*), and a floating clump of variegated spider lily (*Hymenocallis caribaea* 'Variegata') to create a dynamic design, which he then decorated with a flower cut from a water lily (*Nymphaea* spp.).

I'M INTO LITTLE WATER GARDENS in a big way. As the horticulturist responsible for all the displays and plantings in the extensive aquatic gardens flowing through the Denver Botanic Gardens' 23 acres, I find my greatest challenges—and my greatest delights—in designing water gardens for small containers. Over the years, I've learned that a teacup or a half whiskey barrel can house a water garden as exciting as anything I can dream up for the vast, watery canvas at the botanic garden. In fact, small gardens can be even better—they permit you to get close enough to really appreciate the intriguing foliage of the aquatic plants, their spectacular flowers, and their sometimes vibrant scents.

They're foolproof too. If you wind up with a design that you don't like, it's easy to rearrange the plants. Small-container water gardens are actually a collection of submerged potted plants, so redesigning a planting is as simple as moving the pots around. And the plants are tough—most are hard to kill and require little upkeep. All you need is a sunny spot with at least six hours of direct sun a day, something that holds water, and a few plants.

ANYTHING THAT HOLDS WATER CAN BE A WATER GARDEN

The first step in designing a small water garden is deciding on the container. Anything that holds water qualifies. Even if it doesn't, there's still hope—holes can usually be plugged with inexpensive corks to make a container watertight.

I find half barrels to be perfect. At 24 inches wide by 16 inches deep, they are ideally sized to accommodate a dramatic display. The problem, though, is that toxins oozing from the wood can foul both water and plants. So I purchase a durable, plastic liner made to fit perfectly. These are available at many garden centers. Or you could line the barrel with a flexible PVC liner; just be sure to use at least two layers if the material is 10 or fewer millimeters thick; otherwise, the liner will only last a year or two.

Keep design simple; only use a few plants. Tall, spiky plants in the rear provide a dramatic backdrop.

Combine plants with contrasting shapes, colors, and sizes.

Plastic liner protects water and plants from toxins in the wood barrel.

Bricks or empty pots vary the height of plants.

I've also used clay and plastic containers. To keep water from seeping into and through the porous clay of a ceramic container, I apply two coats of sealer. I also use black plastic containers that look like cast-iron pots. I've found them available in three sizes—15, 12, and 9 inches across—and sometimes like displaying them all as a group.

COMPOSE WITH CONTRASTING SHAPES

Water, cupped in a container or basin, is a thing of beauty. Its flickering reflections are a welcome presence in any garden. But dressing it up with plants transports the display to a whole new level. I like to create compositions that are vibrant and dynamic, so I use plants with contrasting shapes, colors, and sizes.

I like to combine the tall, spiky shapes of an erect, fine-leaved marginal plant like yellow flag iris (*Iris pseudacorus*) or sweet flag (*Acorus calamus*) with the broad-leaved foliage of a tropical marginal like taro (*Alocasia* or *Colocasia* spp.). Marginal plants are usually placed along the edges of a water garden; in the wild they grow in shallow water.

For a special touch, I might add a bright splash of color with a cut water lily flower or two. Water lily flowers, which I collect from a larger water garden, will last three days if cut the morning they first open. I don't grow water lilies or lotus in my container compositions, though; they take up too much room. As an especially dramatic accent, I might add a variegated spider lily (*Hymenocallis caribaea* 'Variegata') or a clump of brightly colored

Though water lilies and lotus are usually too big for containers, their cut flowers will last for several days and can be floated in a pot.

Promising Plants for Container Water Gardens

Designing successful container water gardens is a matter of knowing which aquatic plants to use. The following list of plants have worked well for me. Please note that, depending on your climate, some of these aquatic plants can be invasive and should be used *only* in containers.

FANTASTIC FLOATERS

Water lettuce (*Pistia stratiotes*)—This palm-sized plant has soft, wrinkled, light green leaves with a velvety texture. It tolerates more shade than many aquatic plants but may not survive a frost. Can be invasive.

gated sweet flag (*Acorus calamus* 'Variegatus'). Hardy to Zone 4.

Prairie cordgrass (*Spartina pectinata*)—The rugged, grassy foliage grows to about 5 feet high. It sways in the breeze and turns golden brown in late summer. Hardy to Zone 5.

Dwarf papyrus (*Cyperus haspan*)—This plant has bell-shaped flower clusters atop slightly drooping, 18- to 24-inch stems. Hardy to Zone 9.

Cattail (*Typha laxmannii*)—This species has graceful, 4-foot spires of foliage topped, in late summer, by easily recognized

Chameleon plant—*Houttuynia cordata* 'Chameleon'.

Yellow pitcher plant—*Sarracenia flava*.

Water hyacinth (*Eichhornia crassipes*)—Characterized by its swollen, balloonlike leaves, this floater has lilac-blue, irislike flowers that bloom about 6 inches above the water's surface. This tropical and subtropical plant will not survive freezing temperatures. Can be invasive.

Floating moss (*Salvinia rotundifolia*)—This minute-but-exquisite floater has ¾-inch leaves and is ideal for small container water gardens. It may not survive frost.

PLANTS WITH VERTICAL FOLIAGE

Sweet flag (*Acorus calamus*)—The irislike foliage of this grassy plant grows 2 to 4 feet tall and, when broken, releases an invigorating, fruity fragrance. For more color, try white varie-

brown flowers that look like a link of sausage. A dwarf variety, *T. minima* 'Europa', is well-suited to small containers. Grows in Zones 3 to 10.

CASCADING PLANTS

Water mint (*Mentha aquatica*)—This fast-growing plant has fuzzy, roundish leaves that may be reddish-purple in full sun. Its foliage is fragrant when crushed. The plant bears a profusion of tiny, powder-blue flowers. Hardy to Zone 6.

Parrot feather (*Myriophyllum aquaticum*)—As the common name suggests, this is a plant with soft, feathery tufts of foliage. Parrot feather is invasive; check local restrictions on planting in your area. Grows in Zones 6 to 10.

BROAD-LEAVED PLANTS

Taro (*Alocasia* or *Colocasia* spp.)—Excellent water-garden plants with huge leaves that contrast dramatically with slender-foliaged, upright plants. Some varieties have deep burgundy-colored or variegated leaves. It grows to about 3½ feet high. Thrives in Zones 9 and 10.

Canna (*Canna* cvs)—These big-leaved tropicals are available in foliage colors ranging from deep green to purple and pink, with some varieties, especially 'Pretoria', displaying a striking, striped variegation. Heights range from 2 or 3 feet to about 6 feet. Flowers bloom in shades of red, yellow, pink, or orange. Hardy to Zone 7.

Giant arrowhead (*Sagittaria latifolia*)—This easily grown American native has three-petaled white flowers and impressive arrowhead-shaped leaves. It grows up to 4 feet tall and thrives in Zones 5 to 10.

Calla lily (*Zantedeschia aethiopica*)—This plant has arrowhead-shaped leaves and lovely flowers—actually, they're spathes—available in a rainbow of pastel hues. It grows to 2 feet, and is hardy in Zones 9 and 10. For a variety with white-flecked leaves, try *Z. albomaculata*.

MAGICAL MARGINALS: PLANTS THAT DRESS UP A WATER GARDEN

Variegated spider lily (*Hymenocallis caribaea* 'Variegata')—This one will make eyes pop with its electric variegated green and white leaves. It also produces exotic, fragrant, white blooms. Hardy to Zone 8.

Chameleon plant (*Houttuynia cordata* 'Chameleon')—This fast-spreading plant forms a delightful, distinctive mound of red-, green-, and cream-variegated foliage. It belongs at the front of any display. Hardy to Zone 6.

Yellow pitcher plant (*Sarracenia flava*)—This curiosity has erect, trumpet-shaped, insect-eating leaves that are deeply veined with whites and reds. It will reach 12 inches in height. Hardy to Zone 6.

Water celery (*Oenanthe javanica* 'Flamingo')—This plant has a soothing fragrance and delightful, green-tinged-with-pink foliage. It will grow to slowly cascade over the side of your container. Hardy to Zone 8.

Flowers that resemble irises bloom atop the balloonlike leaves of water hyacinth (*Eichhornia crassipes*).

chameleon plant (*Houttuynia cordata* 'Chameleon'). I like using plants that have a story of their own: pitcher plants (*Sarracenia* spp.), for example, eat insects, digesting small bugs in the recesses of their large, trumpet-shaped leaves.

To finish off a planting, I sprinkle a few small floating plants—like water lettuce (*Pistia stratiotes*) or water hyacinth (*Eichhornia crassipes*)—over the surface of the water. I also might soften the hard edge of the container by letting a cascading plant like water mint (*Mentha aquatica*), with its fragrant foliage and powder-blue flowers, tumble over the side.

Whatever plants I use, I try to keep them in scale with the container. Huge plants spilling out of a tiny container most likely would not create a pleasing effect. There are no strict guidelines to follow, so I just aim for a plant and container combination that looks harmonious and proportionate.

FOR A CRISP LOOK, USE ONLY A FEW PLANTS

The first mistake beginning water gardeners make is jamming too many plants into their container. Though a half barrel-sized container easily accommodates up to four plants potted in 2-gallon pots and a host of floating plants, there's no need to use that many. An overcrowded container often results in designs that are chaotic. It's easiest to make pleasing designs with only two or three plants. As you gain experience, you can graduate to more complicated compositions using greater numbers and varieties of plants.

However many you use, how and where you place plants in the container is of paramount importance. The plants should fit as a unit to create the picture you want. First,

The swordlike foliage of variegated sweet flag (*Acorus calamus* 'Variegatus') and the hooded leaves of a yellow pitcher plant (*Sarracenia flava*) make a pleasing composition.

determine how the planting will be viewed. Designing a container that will be seen from a few directions is a lot easier than making one that's meant to be viewed from all sides.

Unless the container is to be displayed in the round, place a tall, spiky plant at the rear to create a dramatic backdrop. Then use a broad-leaved marginal or two in front or to one side, where their generously sized leaves will contrast sharply with the whiplike fronds of taller plants. Keep it simple; otherwise you risk diminishing the effect. For containers that will be seen from all sides, I put the tall, vertical-leaved plant in the middle and arrange broadleafs on each side.

For either kind of design, I arrange and rearrange the plants until I get the effect I'm looking for. It's easy to change the height and position of plants by perching them on bricks or empty, overturned containers. Most marginals, whether their leaves are thin and vertical or broad and horizontal, give excellent results when their crowns are placed 6 inches or less beneath the water's surface. Only after the main parts have been positioned do I begin adding accents like floating or cascading plants, or for a special touch, an eye-catching specimen.

CONTAINER CARE IS EASY

Once your water garden has been planted, caring for it is a simple matter. If the plants don't seem to be thriving, the problem is probably insufficient light. If that's the case, move the container to a brighter spot. If it's too heavy to lift, remove the plants, empty out the water, move the container, and then rearrange it.

Water plants grow quickly but, even so, I encourage them by using fertilizing tablets. For new plants, I delay fertilizing until they show signs of growth. When a plant gets big, I divide and repot it in heavy clay soil. Dense

Floating plants add a finishing touch. The rippled leaves of water lettuce (*Pistia stratiotes*) make a nice complement to spotted calla (*Zantedeschia albomaculata*) and soft rush (*Juncus effusus*).

soils won't cloud the water when containers are moved, and, just to be sure, I always firm the soil fairly tightly before lowering the container back into the water. If the plants seem too robust, I limit their growth by keeping them in small pots and trimming off the oldest and tallest leaves.

There's no need to change the water in a container garden, although you should top it off every few days to replace liquid that may have evaporated. I've never had problems with mosquitoes breeding in containers, but if you want to eliminate any chance of establishing a breeding ground for insects, you might wash the larvae out by overfilling your container with water or add a few mosquito-fish (*Gambusia affinis)*, voracious eaters that feed on mosquito larvae. Aquatic nurseries have also developed specially formulated products for killing mosquito larvae.

Winter doesn't have to mean the end of the garden. Most water plants can be brought indoors and used as houseplants, kept in an aquarium, or even placed in a tub of water in a cool basement. Hardy plants could be left in the container but may need protection against freezing. Where winters are severe, birdbath-type heaters can prevent your container water garden from turning into a giant ice cube.

When spring comes, plants are usually ready to divide. Use the extras to start a new water garden—by then you'll probably be immersed in the world of aquatic plants.

KEITH CORLETT

is a specialist in terrace and penthouse gardens whose gardens are regularly included on the City Gardens Club and Garden Conservancy tours.

A Penthouse Garden

On a 37th floor rooftop overlooking downtown Manhattan, this garden is an oasis far removed from the bustle of the streets below.

A PENTHOUSE GARDEN TOWERING high above the skyline of Manhattan is the equivalent of Eden for those of us who are garden lovers trapped in the city. It's a tranquil oasis and retreat from the hustle and bustle down below, and the contrast vividly sharpens the appreciation. But creating such a garden is a challenge. Space is at a premium. Building codes prescribe limits on weight and materials. The rooftop climate swings to inhospitable extremes. And all the plants in the garden must grow in containers.

I design, install, and maintain penthouse and terrace gardens in New York. The logistics of the work are tricky. My crew and I have to move all the construction materials, soil, and plants via the elevator, and sometimes via the stairs, to the rooftop. It's a little like dismantling a whole garden at ground level, moving it piece by piece, and reassembling it again on top. The job has to be done

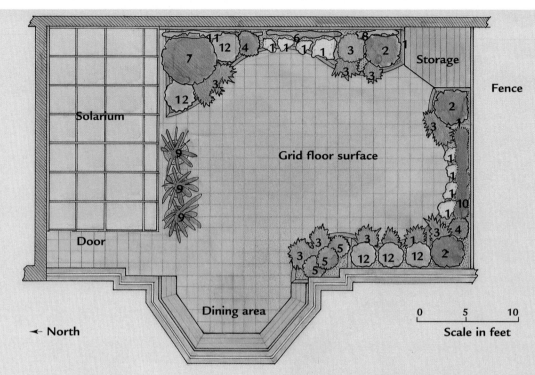

1. Annuals
2. American arborvitae (*Thuja occidentalis*)
3. Dwarf junipers (cvs. of *Juniperus chinensis* and *J. horizontalis*)
4. Lawson false cypress (*Chamaecyparis lawsoniana* 'Minima Aurea')
5. American arborvitae (*Thuja occidentalis* 'Woodwardii')
6. Firethorn (*Pyracantha* 'Mohave')
7. Serbian spruce (*Picea omorika*)
8. Sweet autumn clematis (*Clematis terniflora*)
9. Tropicals (replaced each year)
10. Rocky Mountain juniper (*Juniperus scopulorum* 'Skyrocket')
11. Wisteria (*Wisteria sinensis*)
12. Japanese yews (*Taxus cuspidata* 'Capitata' and 'Intermedia')

quickly and cleanly, and with maximum consideration. There's double-parking on a busy street, blocking the pedestrian sidewalk, hogging the elevator with a mountain of stuff, traipsing through carpeted hallways and through the customer's apartment (usually newly decorated) to the terrace. Making a suburban garden is a breeze by comparison.

As with gardens on the ground, each site poses special problems and opportunities, but I can introduce some of the general principles of rooftop gardening by describing a garden I designed and still maintain.

WORKING WITH LIMITED SPACE

Located near the top of one of New York City's tallest apartment buildings, this garden is about 20 feet wide by 25 feet long, with a small bay that projects out like a balcony. The garden faces west, and is sheltered on the east side by the wall of the building. On the north end, a 9-foot by 16-foot solarium makes a transition into the interior of the apartment.

This postage stamp–size garden serves as an outdoor room for summer living and entertaining. I wanted to create the appearance of lushness without crowding out the

people, so I designed cedar planters that cover a minimum (about 10 percent) of the limited floor space, and used tall, narrow trees and vines to create maximum impact with the vertical space.

The planters are either 18 inches or 24 inches high and 2 feet to 6 feet wide and long. They need to be this big to hold enough soil for the number and size of the plants included. Because the plants are relatively large for their containers and because they're crowded together, the foliage mass is significantly (though deliberately) out of proportion to the soil mass. I filled the planters with a mixture of one part topsoil for root anchoring and normal biological activity, one part peat moss for friability and moisture retention, and one part vermiculite for aeration and porosity. The peat moss and vermiculite also lighten the soil mix. Altogether, the weight of planters, soil, and plants must be within the load limit imposed by city building codes, but this usually isn't a problem.

CONFRONTING THE ROOFTOP CLIMATE

Weather is exaggerated on a rooftop. During the course of a year, the temperature can vary up to 130°F. It gets both cooler and hotter than on the ground below. Street-level Manhattan is rated as USDA Zone 7, but climbing 37 floors above the moderating effect of the ground gives the equivalent of Zone 4 conditions (-20° to -30°F) in winter. Conversely, in the summer, if the temperature at street level is 80° to 90°F, it will be 10° to 20°F hotter up above, as heat reflects off the surrounding buildings. It's good to have at least half a day's shade to moderate the summer heat. This garden gets no sun until after noon.

Moisture supply is another problem on a rooftop. Average annual rainfall here is about 42 inches. Much of that would soak into the soil of a ground-level garden, and be available for plant roots. On a rooftop, though, most of the rainfall is lost as runoff. The amount of rainwater that soaks into the soil in the containers is much less than would be available to plants growing in the ground.

In addition, the drying effect of extreme temperatures and winds is a real threat to rooftop plants. They bake-dry in the summer and freeze-dry in the winter—alternately experiencing both desert and tundra conditions. Wind tunneling between surrounding buildings can reach speeds of 60 mph at any time of the year.

To create an effect of maximum greenery without filling valuable floor space, Corlett planted pyracantha, wisteria, and clematis vines, and trained them against a wall on the east side of the garden area.

"Most important is selecting plants that are slow-growing and tolerate crowding, and that are hardy to at least three climate zones north of your location."

An automatic watering system is a necessity. It reduces stress on the plants and relieves the owner of this chore. The garden can go without attention for days, weeks, or months if necessary. I installed a drip system on this job. In the summer, it turns on at least twice a day, since the limited soil mass in the planters can't hold a full day's supply of water. In the winter, I turn the system off and drain it so it won't freeze. Natural precipitation is enough to support the plants during the dormant season.

All rooftops and terraces, whether or not they incorporate a garden, are equipped with drains to carry off the runoff from natural rainfall, which far exceeds the runoff from a drip-irrigation system. In a controlled drip system adjusted for each planter's needs, only 5 percent of the irrigation water runs off. When a rooftop garden is installed, the drain must be kept clear at all times, since the watering system or the garden is (alas) always singled out as the culprit for roof leaks.

CONIFERS SURVIVE CONDITIONS

Only tough, adaptable plants tolerate the weather extremes atop a skyscraper. Conifers do much better than do most deciduous trees and shrubs in these conditions, so I used them extensively in this garden. I chose plants that are cold-hardy beyond Zone 4, and they've survived even though the soil in the planters freezes solid in the winter. They can also withstand the cold and wind above ground. Some years the arborvitae (*Thuja occidentalis*) and false cypresses (*Chamaecyparis lawsoniana*) get browned by windburn, but the junipers (*Juniperus* spp.), spruces (*Picea omorika*), and yews (*Taxus* spp.) all hold up pretty well. It's possible to grow less-hardy evergreens with special care, but I don't bother, since antidesiccants would have to be applied at least twice during the winter, when the temperature was above 50°F, and it's hard to schedule a job like that. Wrapping less-hardy trees with burlap would protect them, but that would look ugly, and this garden is meant to be seen year-round.

Conifers tolerate the high winds on a rooftop. Unlike deciduous trees, which usu-

Modular Planters

Everything in a rooftop garden has to be movable in case the roof itself needs maintenance, so the planters I designed are made of several separate freestanding sections. Two men can move a planter, even when it's filled with soil and plants. A facade of vertical boards runs along the front of all the sections to give the appearance of one continuous, graceful curve.

The facade reaches down to the floor, but the bottoms of the actual containers are supported by 2x4s laid on edge, to maintain an air space underneath. That air space is essential for keeping roots from growing down out of the drain holes in the bottom of the containers. Needless to say, there's trouble if roots penetrate into a roof. I've seen places where an undetected tree root lifted a row of tiles all the way across a roof in a single season.

ally have a trunk with a heavy mass of foliage at the top, conifers distribute their foliage more evenly from top to bottom. This lower center of gravity is more stable; also, conifer needles present less wind drag than deciduous leaves do. Some of the junipers and arborvitae are 8 feet tall, but I don't have to stake or tie them to keep them steady and upright. Another attribute of conifers is that, unlike some broadleaved trees, their limbs rarely break off in storms.

Conifers have other advantages in a rooftop garden. They provide a variety of size, shape, texture, and foliage color year-round. They're slow growing, so they don't quickly overrun the design, and they don't have aggressive root systems that outgrow their containers. They tolerate crowding without contracting the fungal diseases that plague many herbaceous and deciduous plants, and they require minimal maintenance. They don't need much pruning, and they don't drop a lot of litter.

To complete the design, I planted pyracantha, wisteria, and clematis against the wall on the east side of the garden. The pyracantha (*Pyracantha* 'Mohave'), a woody plant with small evergreen leaves and bright red berries in the fall and winter, is trained as an espalier. The wisteria (*Wisteria sinensis*) climbs on wires. Unchecked, it would rapidly take over the whole garden, but I prune it severely twice a year, in November and late February, which also stimulates flower production. The sweet autumn clematis (*Clematis terniflora*) dies back to the ground each winter, but quickly fills its space in the summer. It needs only a bit of encouragement to stay in place on the wires against the wall.

In late spring, I plant a few annuals for some additional color. Impatiens and salvias work well because they flower from spring to

frost and can tolerate crowding without succumbing to fungal problems. Geraniums (*Pelargonium* spp.) and dusty miller (*Senecio viravira*) are other long-lasting annuals. In rooftop gardens, perennials don't tend to fare well, as they're too vulnerable to winter cold and too susceptible to fungal diseases when cramped. After frost in the fall, I discard the annuals and clean up the garden for the winter.

Ground-level rules don't apply on a rooftop, and it's a challenge to cope with these difficult conditions. Most important is selecting plants that are slow-growing and tolerate crowding, and that are hardy to at least three climate zones north of your location. I generally install mature plants, as they have the best chance of surviving the adversity and competition. But, of course, before I can plant them on the roof, they first have to fit in the elevator. That's the key to almost everything I do.

Conifers are ideal plants for rooftop containers. They provide a variety of foliage colors and textures, are interesting to look at in all seasons, and tolerate extreme heat, cold, and winds. This garden includes yews, globe arborvitae, and dwarf junipers.

The Art *of* Container *Gardening*

MICHAEL BOWELL

is the owner of Flora Design Associates, which specializes in indoor and outdoor garden design, in West Chester, Pennsylvania.

A cascading container planting designed by the author helps to give a feeling of enclosure for a pool area. The composition builds upward from purple verbena to white petunias and blue salvia, capped off with a 'Pink Delight' butterfly bush.

WHEN I DESCRIBE MY PLANS for a container garden to a client, I find myself walking around the imaginary cluster of pots to show how they will fill the space, while indicating with my arms the topography created by plants of different heights. And with my hands I explain the shapes and textures that will soon give the spark of life to a deck or patio.

What need is there for such body language? If it's a simple pot of geraniums (*Pelargonium*, spp.) you want, there isn't any. But if you want something more, then you must think in terms of height, texture, and shape, as well as color, when selecting your plants and containers. Many gardeners think of container gardens as static creations: Pop in a few annuals, give them a little water, then stand back and wait for color. I think of container plantings as flower arrangements that change throughout the season.

My containers are not low maintenance. I aim for an attractive display from earliest spring to late fall, so I plant and transplant, pinch and train, all season long. I enjoy the control I have over these tiny gardens, control I don't have over any other part of my 5-acre property. You may not have the time or the energy to exercise the same kind of control over your containers, but you can borrow some principles of design and choice of plants from my containers and improve the looks of your potted arrangements.

ASSEMBLING THE PIECES

Designing a container garden is a matter of arranging plants in a way that is both artistically pleasing and suited to the health of the plants. I start by visualizing the role that the planting will play. Container plantings can extend the ground level garden up steps or onto a patio as a transition from flowing plant forms to the hardness of concrete, wood, or brick. Container plantings also can be used either to attract or to distract the viewer's eye. Two containers placed a short distance from one another can frame a view and, at the same time, direct the eye away from something visually less appealing. Container plantings arranged around a sitting area or a hot tub can serve either as a backdrop or as a screen.

Once you've determined the container garden's role in the landscape, think about the architecture of the plantings. Consider height, width, and depth to keep your living sculpture from fading into the two-dimensional background. In my containers I use pieces of old bittersweet or grapevines, as

Group containers together for a dynamic display. Larger plants in the background draw the eye upward, creating vertical movement. Support vines, such as mandevilla, with stakes or poles. Cascading plants hide pots.

An urn of petunias, New Guinea impatiens, and begonias welcomes visitors with a harmonious mix of soft pinks.

"Look for plants that are tough in the face of thunder showers, heat waves, and insect pests; that look good all season long; and that bear flowers that show up well from a distance."

flower arrangers do, to bring the eye up, out of the container, and then back down. Living vines can serve as either a vertical or a trailing element. In containers near walls I sometimes train more than one vine out of the pot at various angles on fishing line, creating cozy niches for patio chairs. I also like to fill containers with plants of varying heights and with plants that grow to different sizes over the course of the season. The arching stems of lilies, for example, pop out over lower-growing plants and explode with color.

Before choosing plants for a container garden, select the vessel itself. There are as many different possible containers as there are types of plants to put in them. In general, I try to match containers to their surroundings. In a formal setting, classical stone urns may be appropriate. In an informal setting—at a country house, for example—wood or terra-cotta would be good choices.

I rarely use one container alone. One is not usually enough for a successful composition. I use two, three, or more pots in clusters—larger containers toward the back and smaller ones in front. Placed this way, the plants go from ground level to eye level and beyond, creating vertical movement and a cascading effect. I also tuck small containers into large ones. For example, to perk up a flagging display, you can set a flowering orchid or a budding perennial lily, still in its pot, on top of the soil of a larger pot, instantly integrating it into the scheme of your arrangement. The leaves of the other plants camouflage the pot.

When you are ready to choose plants for your containers, keep contrast in mind. Contrast is the dynamism of the planting, creating a rhythmic flow for the eye to follow. A container isn't interesting if all you see is a blur. I always strive for strong contrast in the sizes of plants, their shapes and their leaf textures.

There will always be heated debates about which color combinations are successful and

Contrasting shapes, textures, and foliage colors enliven container plantings. The silvery, cut leaves of dusty miller (*Senecio viravira*) set off the bolder foliage of geraniums, *verbena*, pinks (*Dianthus* spp), petunias, and cockscomb (*Celosia*, spp.).

The warm colors of 'Mini Balcomb Coral' geranium, 'Peter Pan Flame' zinnia, and yellow *Zinnia linearis*, complemented by blue mealycup sage (*Salvia farinacea* 'Victoria'), catch the eye from a distance.

even trees can do very well in large pots or tubs. Making use of such unexpected plants allows you to design incredibly varied and dynamic plantings.

Including bulbs, perennials, and woody plants in a container garden does require some extra effort, though. In cold-winter climates such as we have here in southeastern Pennsylvania (USDA Zone 6), many plants that are perfectly hardy in the ground will perish if left outdoors in a pot. These plants make for very expensive annuals; to ensure their survival for next year's container plantings, transplant them into the ground in the fall.

I put some unusual plants in my containers, but many of the plants I use are uncommon cultivars of traditional favorites. I experiment extensively with different varieties of all sorts of plants. I also go to trial gardens at universities or botanical gardens to see how new cultivars are faring in our area. In general, I look for plants that are tough in the face of thunder showers, heat waves, and insect pests, that look good all season long, and that bear flowers that show up well from a distance. I also look for unusual colors in flowers or foliage for the variety they add to a color scheme. I often use my own containers as a laboratory. If a new variety consistently out performs an old one, I begin to use it in all my plantings.

You may have to hunt a little to find uncommon plants. Because of the volume of my business, I can have plants custom grown by local nurseries. But I also grow a number of out-of-the-ordinary plants from seed.

I usually order seed of particular varieties in a single color, but I also try mixes every year. I always find a color shade in the mix that isn't available as a single color variety.

which aren't. In the end, it's a matter of personal taste. Do whatever works for you, but remember that in a container garden, the colors are concentrated and viewed at close hand. The same combinations that blend harmoniously in a meadow can be visual cacophony in a planter box that sits a few feet from your front door. Aim for a mixture of softer colors for areas near where people sit. Use hotter colors in containers that are farther from view.

CHOOSING PLANTS

Many gardeners limit their container plant palette to the same old annuals. Don't! Open your mind to the enormous range of plants that can thrive in containers. I'll use anything in a container: Bulbs, perennials, shrubs, and

A Selection of Favorites

To give a better idea of how I choose plants and combine them, I've picked out a few of my favorites. Some of these will be familiar to you; others will be new. If you can't find the exact plant I recommend, try another, similar one. The important thing is to experiment.

SWAN RIVER DAISY

(*Brachyscome iberidifolia*)—This prostrate, thread-leaved annual produces myriads of small, purple daisies in all but the hottest weather and carries on until hard frost. It looks great trailing over the side of a container where it makes a nice contrast to the bolder flowers of cup flower (*Nierembergia caerulea* 'Purple Robe') or the feathery blue of floss flower (*Ageratum* spp.). I buy it, as I do many annuals, in hanging baskets from a local garden center. These baskets appear to be more expensive than six-packs, but when you see the size of the six-odd plants you get when you pull the clump apart, you'll realize that you're getting a deal.

HONEYSUCKLE FUCHSIA

(*Fuchsia* 'Gartenmeister Bonstedt')—Unlike the trailing fuchsia you see in hanging pots, this one has an upright growth habit, reaching 18 to 24 inches tall. You can grow it alone as a specimen plant; its salmon-orange flowers go beautifully with its bronzy foliage. But the honeysuckle fuchsia also combines well with other plants. Try it with the similarly warm colors of a golden variegated ivy or coral multiflora petunias. For a cooler, tapestried effect, combine it with purple petunias (*Petunia* hybrids). The honeysuckle fuchsia takes hot sun well, but will also tolerate shade. It flowers all season long, right up to cold weather. Like its namesake, the honeysuckle fuchsia also attracts hummingbirds.

BLEEDING HEART

(*Dicentra spectabilis*)—The old-fashioned bleeding heart makes a great early-to-midseason container plant. It flow-ers prolifically for me from mid-April through early July. When it starts to fade, I cut it to the soil level and fill in around it with annuals. In the fall, I dig up the roots and overwinter them in the ground. In the spring, I lift them and put them back in a container. Combine bleeding hearts with tulips (*Tulipa* spp.), buttercups (*Ranunculus* spp.), pansies, and *Lobelia* for an early-season container. Include some cold-tolerant mainstays of the summer garden, such as *Verbena*, to fill in as the cool-season plants fade.

BUTTERFLY BUSH

(*Buddleja davidii*)—There are a number of butterfly bush cultivars from which to choose. I particularly like 'Pink Delight'. The long-lasting pink flower spikes go nicely with tall verbena (*Verbena bonariensis*), a wonderfully tall "see-through" plant topped with clusters of lavender-mauve flowers. I use butterfly bush year after year in some of my larger containers where its 5 to 6-foot size provides adequate height and mass. I overwinter the plants, which are hardy to Zone 5, in the ground, pruning them back hard each spring to keep them in scale. If a butterfly bush gets too large, I either find a spot for it in the garden or I "bonsai" it—controlling its size by severely pruning both roots and top.

MANDEVILLA

(*Mandevilla* × *amoera* 'Alice du Pont')—I recommend this cultivar for its 3-inch wide, pink trumpet flowers that stand out in a crowded planter. I train this fast-growing tropical vine up stakes, up a pole, or up a wall. 'Alice duPont' adds height to a pink container planting. Try it with *Verbena* 'Sissinghurst Pink' or the annual Madagascar periwinkle (*Catharanthus roseus*) such as 'Pretty in Pink'. It also looks good in a mass of vines, combining well with the smaller flowers of its neighbors. I love it with the purple-veined foliage, pink, sweet pea-like flowers and bright purple seedpods of the hyacinth bean (*Lablab purpureus*).

Potted Plantings in the Shade

GARY KEIM

is a garden designer, horticultural consultant, writer, and editor. Previously a designer at Longwood Gardens, he gardens near Philadelphia.

Many plants perform well in pots in shady places. Although the terrace garden receives less than three hours of sun a day, it hosts an array of brightly colored plants.

JUST WHEN I GET MY GARDENING routine down pat, new challenges arise to test my knowledge or shatter my perceptions. Such was the case when I moved from my previous garden—which had an open exposure bathed in sun from morning to sundown—to a garden overshadowed by tall trees. My new gardening venue is a bluestone terrace surrounded by a mixed woods of tulip tree, American ash, and white oak. The 100-foot-high canopy is especially heavy on the south side, casting shade for most of the day. I wanted to make this terrace a home for a collection of potted plants, but I was skeptical about what would do well there.

I've since realized that container gardening in the shade offers numerous benefits. Shaded pots don't dry out as fast as ones baking in full sun, so watering is less of a chore. Of course, with plants growing in pots there's no competition from tree roots, which is often the case with shade gardening. Best of all, I've discovered wonderful new plants and different ways to combine them.

LOOK FOR ZESTY FORMS OF OLD STANDARDS

Being a fan of the new and different when it comes to plants, I was tempted to disregard the standard repertoire of shade-loving plants—begonias, impatiens, and coleus. But then I remembered that it's how plants are used that makes them special. With a little hunting, I found striking cultivars of each. They provided eye-catching color and set the mood for my container vignettes.

One of my favorite discoveries was *Begonia* 'Dragon Wings Hybrid'. This fibrous-rooted begonia has shiny, medium green leaves and dangling red blossoms borne in clusters at the ends of arching stems. While it can be

Some begonias boast exceptional foliage and flowers. The shiny green leaves of Begonia *'Dragon Wings Hybrid' are accented by dangling clusters of red blooms.*

likened to a wax-leaved begonia, its lax habit and stature set it apart. I grew it in black-painted, cast-iron urns, combining it with white-variegated flax lily (*Dianella tasmanica* 'Variegata') in the urn's center and variegated ground ivy (*Glechoma hederacea* 'Variegata') spilling down the sides in long chains of foliage.

I found two exceptional selections of double impatiens. 'Pink Ice' boasts variegated foliage and salmon-pink flowers. The cultivar 'Red' of the Rose Parade Series produces deep red blooms in great profusion. As a solo planting, it accented a pairing of pots with a red-and-pink color scheme. These larger pots featured a pink-and-green selection of coleus, *Lobelia* 'Queen Victoria', *Fuchsia* 'Gartenmeister Bonstedt', *Lamium maculatum* 'White Nancy', variegated ground ivy, *Hosta* 'Patriot', and variegated lilyturf (*Ophiopogon jaburan* 'Vittatus').

Nearly every grouping of pots showcased coleus. With the explosion of new coleus available, there's a cultivar to fit almost any color scheme. Their leaves vary from a single, solid hue to a complex mix of colors. One such planting featured a large pot of coleus (a sport of 'The Line'), which I carry over from year to year as cuttings. It anchored a grouping of yellow-leaved plants accented by ones with orange, apricot, and salmon flowers.

DON'T BE AFRAID TO EXPERIMENT

Although in general I looked for plants known to thrive in shade, there were a few sun-lovers I just didn't want to give up. Some, such as angel's trumpets (*Brugmansia* 'Jamaican Yellow'), fared well. Plants that require prolonged intense sun, such as Petunia hybrids, lavenders (*Lavendula* spp.), and curry plant (*Helichrysum italicum*), did not. And herein lies a valuable lesson: Each shady site is different, so experimentation is the only way to know for sure what will do well in a given situation.

To my surprise, *Canna* 'Durban' grew well and even bloomed. Of course, even if this canna had never bloomed, its intricately veined, green-and-yellow leaves alone would have warranted its cultivation. Yellow-variegated American aloe (*Agave americana*) held its own, even growing slightly through the season. Pinwheel (*Aeonium haworthii*) and mescal (*Agave parryi*), both succulents, grew well and added their blue note of foliage interest. These made a stunning picture when combined with a selection of hot water plants (*Achimenes* cvs.).

FOLIAGE CAN ADD STRUCTURE AND COLOR

More than anything else, foliage gives body to container groupings. It provides the backbone and adds color to reinforce the floral display. I think variegated plants are invaluable in shade gardening; they brighten up shadowy areas, and their leaf colors and patterns relieve the monotony of green.

One of my groupings relied solely on foliage for impact. At its center was a *Begonia* 'Exotica', a variegated begonia that lives up to its name. Its leaves are olive-green with deep pink blotches and a metallic sheen. The thin, deep maroon leaves of blood leaf (*Iresine lindenii*) offered textural contrast, and *Caladium bicolor* 'Rosalie'—with deep-red-centered leaves edged in green—echoed the blood leaf. A lone red impatiens added a bit of floral color while reinforcing the red theme. A young specimen of a lacecap hydrangea (*Hydrangea macrophylla*

'Mariesii'), with its white-edged leaves, added contrast to this somewhat monochromatic scheme.

I'm glad I've discovered the rewards of gardening with potted plants in the shade. Now I'm excited about the countless possibilities for what I might grow on my terrace next season.

Plants with vibrant leaves enliven shaded areas. A lime-green coleus anchors this grouping of similarly hued foliage plants.

"Experimentation is the only way to know for sure what will do well in a given situation."

DESIGNING
CONTAINER PLANTINGS

2

BECAUSE CONTAINER GARDENS ALLOW you the convenience of small-scale gardening, you can assemble a dozen small but very different gardens with minimal effort. Few plants perform well from spring through fall and into the winter, but you can easily rearrange your container gardens with the changing of the seasons.

The trick is to create a great combination of plants—whether you're combining pots of plants or creating a mixed planting in a single container. And for that you need a good design. Fortunately, following a few simple guidelines will enable you to create great container gardens. Our contributors share some of their favorite combinations and explain why they work. You may want to try some of these, or perhaps they'll inspire you to come up with stunning combinations of your own.

Creative Plant

Combinations

SYDNEY EDDISON

is a long-time contributor
to *Fine Gardening*. She
has written numerous
gardening books,
including *The Self-Taught
Gardener*.

Group different-sized
containers for a
satisfying arrangement.
Here, plectranthus
plays a starring role.

GROWING ATTRACTIVE PLANT combinations out-of-doors in containers becomes more appealing to me every year. For a fraction of the effort in preparing even a small flower bed, you can make a dozen container gardens. Besides saving physical wear and tear, it liberates your imagination and fosters experimentation.

You can make arrangements by using a single plant in each container and assembling the containers in a satisfying way, or by combining plants in one large container. There is ample room in a barrel for a half dozen plants; an 18-inch urn or pot can comfortably accommodate three or four plants.

Conventional containers include pots of clay or plastic, wooden window boxes, and half whiskey barrels. But anything that will hold 6 to 8 inches of soil and has plenty of drainage holes can be employed. I'm not partial to

Purple spiderwort contasts with yellow lantana and hardy yucca. Licorice plant softens container edges. The spiderwort weaves through the licorice plant, filling in any empty spaces.

This recipe results in a rich, full effect, like an overflowing cornucopia. In the back of my mind are the huge flower bouquets in the lobby of The Metropolitan Museum of Art in New York. Arching fountains of branches, flowers, and foliage fill matching niches on either side of the entrance. Lush but not unruly, elegant but not stiff.

Annuals and tender perennials offer a fantastic range of container subjects, but some hardy perennials also make good additions. I love ornamental grasses and hardy yucca as focal points. Just remember to rescue them before winter. Remove them from the pots, and plant them in the ground. They can be repotted in spring. Dormant perennials are easily damaged if water accumulates in the pot and freezes.

CONTRAST COLOR AND FORM

One of my favorite combinations last summer was a trio of tender perennials—purple-leaved spiderwort (*Tradescantia pallida* 'Purple Heart'), licorice plant (*Helichrysum petiolare* 'Limelight'), and shrubby lantana (*Lantana camara*)—accented by the stiff, bright yellow and green swords of hardy yucca (*Yucca filamentosa* 'Variegata'). Together, these plants made a jazzy yellow-and-purple color scheme that everybody admired.

The 'Purple Heart' spiderwort, so named for its gorgeous dusky foliage, has jointed stems that stand up on their own or trail over the edge of a container. As a bonus, the terminal shoots produce small, triangular, mauve-pink flowers. In this combination, the dark, leafy stems wove in and out among the light chartreuse leaves of the licorice plant and the green-and-yellow variegated leaves of lantana.

weird containers, but wire and wicker baskets with coco-fiber liners can be charming. And if you have an old stone sink or trough, you are just plain lucky.

START WITH A STAR-QUALITY PLANT

There are as many ways to plant containers as there are gardeners who enjoy the challenge, but I have arrived at a formula that seems to work for a large pot. You need one big plant with real star quality for a centerpiece; one or two soft, billowy plants that will not object to being crowded and will weave through the centerpiece; a stiff, spiky plant that provides height and strong lines; and a trailing plant or two to blur the container's sharp edges.

One year, I planted this same container more simply with a tall sheaf of ruby chard (*Beta vulgaris* 'Ruby Chard') in the middle. Then I stuck in seeds of 'Alaska Hybrid' nasturtium (*Tropaeolum majus* 'Alaska Hybrid'). By midsummer, the deep green leaves of the ruby chard with their scarlet midribs were surrounded by red and orange nasturtiums with variegated green-and-white leaves.

Another year, the centerpiece was a clump of annual fountain grass (*Pennisetum setaceum* 'Rubrum') with narrow, dark red blades and fuzzy, caterpillar seed heads hedged in by brilliant orange dwarf marigolds (*Tagetes* 'Janie Tangerine'). The edge of the pot was softened by beautiful masses of golden oregano (*Origanum vulgare* 'Aureum').

DON'T OVERPLANT YOUR CONTAINERS

Over the years, I have learned that three kinds of plants provide enough variety in a single container. This is not counting ivy and vinca, which take up so little space they can be squeezed in anywhere as trailers. But I have often gotten carried away and jammed in too many plants with different growth rates. As a result, the weaker plants became swamped by the more aggressive subjects. It is better to start with three relatively vigorous growers and keep them under control by cutting them back when necessary.

Grooming makes the difference between a beautiful container display and a mess. Don't hesitate to trim vines or other trailing plants to limit their growth and keep them neat. Also, removing the dead flowers from annuals not only makes them look better, it keeps them flowering.

Designing containers for the terrace is one of my favorite forms of gardening. While a perennial garden remains more or less the

Three different plants are enough per container for season-long visual interest.

Coleus and canna make fanciful partners. Canna stars as the centerpiece, while coleus blurs the container edges.

same year after year, a container garden presents you with a fresh, new canvas every season. And you can indulge your wildest notions because you are never stuck with your failures. In the fall, the annuals and tender perennials succumb to frost anyway. Next year, you can try something new.

B. B. STAMATS

B. B Stamats runs a landscape design and installation business in Ridgefield, Connecticut. She also lectures on container gardening.

Planting for All-Season Interest

Place all-season pots in borders throughout the year. In winter, potted conifers look dramatic coated with snow.

THE SEASON FOR OUTDOOR container gardening doesn't have to end when deep freezes make mush of coleus. Pots with winter-hardy plants can be versatile players throughout the garden. These same containers can be jazzed up in other seasons with the addition of less-hardy plants.

In 10 years of experimenting with all-season containers, I've confronted the special challenges winter poses to keeping plants healthy and attractive. The key to all-season container plantings is making sure that both pots and plants can withstand the most inclement weather they're likely to endure. Where I live in southwestern Connecticut (Zone 6), this means protecting them from freezes, heavy winds, and other wintry hazards. Basically, this involves selecting appropriate plants and containers,

Spruce up winter-hardy plantings with annuals. In this summery combination, white-flowering begonias nestle above juniper while dried branches of Harry Lauder's walking stick add height.

paying careful attention to where they're placed, and providing timely maintenance.

While the plant palette is more limited in winter, there are still many exciting options. Plants most likely to survive severe weather in pots are drought-resistant broadleaved evergreens and conifers. I also enjoy the architectural forms of deciduous trees and shrubs, especially when they are highlighted by a coating of snow.

Remember that some plant varieties are hardier than others. For example, I've had better luck with green-leaved cutleaf Japanese maple cultivars (*Acer palmatum*) than red-leaved ones. Also, I've found that some plants simply do not overwinter well in my climate. In general, choose plants that are one or two zones hardier than your location.

FROSTPROOF POTS WORK BEST

In blustery-cold climates, the containers themselves must withstand freezing temperatures. To avert cracking when subjected to freezing, terra-cotta or concrete pots must be at least 1½ to 2 inches thick. However, their bulkiness makes them hard to move.

Recently, there's been an explosion in the availability of lightweight, freeze-resistant containers made from fiberglass, polyethylene, and structural foam. These pots insulate the soil, which helps regulate the temperature and retain moisture better than traditional pots. I also like the ease with which I can move these containers. In general, I recommend using large pots—at least 22 inches high and 24 inches wide—since the volume of soil they hold further insulates plant roots.

To plant trees and shrubs. I first place polystyrene peanuts in the bottom quarter of the pot to lighten the pot's weight. With newly purchased plants, I then examine the roots. If they're root-bound, I make four to six 1-inch cuts with my pruners, slicing vertically from top to bottom. For a potting mix, I use one part sterile topsoil with two parts sterile potting soil. I also use a fertilizer specified for either conifers or deciduous shrubs. I water thoroughly, then top off the pot with 2 inches of shredded hardwood mulch to hold moisture and insulate the soil.

GIVE POTS SOME SHELTER

If possible, protect your container plantings from the prevailing winter winds. Your home or a dense hedge—preferably evergreen—can serve as a good wind screen. When choosing a location, keep in mind that sheltered, north-facing areas are actually less punishing than southern or eastern exposures, which warm by day and drop quickly to freezing temperatures by night. This freeze-and-thaw cycle can severely damage plants.

To create variations of form, color, and texture, I group several pots together. For example, I may arrange three pots of plants of varying heights in a triangle. During the warmer months, I often move my pots with evergreen plants to other locations, as statuesque plants can add structure to a perennial border. Or, I plant annuals within the all-season container. While it takes a bit more work, I sometimes move my winter plants into nursery pots or to a garden bed for the summer and use the decorative pots for other plantings.

WATER, EVEN IN WINTER

Plants grown in pots are more vulnerable to winter damage than the same plants grown in the ground. The most critical challenge is to avoid letting a plant's roots dry out. As feeder roots freeze, they stop absorbing water. To give my plants a head start as winter approaches, I make sure I keep pots watered well until the first hard freeze. I also check to make sure the pots drain well. From November through March, whenever the temperature rises above 40°F, I check plants for moisture and, when they're dry, I add cold water. During the rest of the year, I water as needed to keep plants from drying out. I fertilize winter pots each spring and repot them every two to three years.

By Thanksgiving, I spray antidesiccants on my evergreen plants, except on those which, according to product instructions, may be adversely affected. I repeat this treatment every six to seven weeks. When it snows, I gently remove the snow from branches but let it melt into the pots. During the rest of the winter, I simply enjoy seeing the plantings from outdoors and inside.

Plant Picks for All Season Pots

These plants are recommended for year-round outdoor containers.

EVERGREEN PLANTS	ZONE
Common boxwood (*Buxus sempervirens*)	Zones 5-8
Dwarf and semidwarf pines (*Pinus* spp. and cultivars)	Zones 2-8
Dwarf arborvitaes (*Thuja* varieties and cultivars)	Zones 2-8
Dwarf golden juniper (*Juniperis communis* 'Depressa Aurea')	Zones 2-6
Dwarf hemlocks (*Tsuga* varieties and cultivars)	Zones 4-7
Dwarf spruces (*Picea* varieties and cultivars)	Zones 2-7
English yew (*Taxus baccata*)	Zones 6-7
Golden Japanese false cypress (*Chamaecyparis pisifera* 'Filifera Aurea')	Zones 4-8
Japanese pieris (*Pieris japonica*)	Zones 5-8
Mountain laurel (*Kalmia latifolia*)	Zones 4-9
Siberian cypress (*Microbiota decussata*)	Zones 3-7
Single-seed juniper (*Juniperis squamata*)	Zones 4-7
Wintercreeper (*Euonymous fortunei*)	Zones 5-8
'Wintergreen' Japanese umbrella pine (*Sciadopitys verticillata* 'Wintergreen')	Zones 5-9

DECIDUOUS PLANTS	
Downy serviceberry (*Amelanchier arborea*)	Zones 4-9
Dwarf fothergilla (*Fothergilla gardenii*)	Zones 5-9
Harry Lauder's walking stick (*Corylus avellana* 'Contorta')	Zones 4-8
'Nana' winterberry (*Ilex verticillata* 'Nana')	Zones 3-9
PeeGee hydrangea (*Hydrangea paniculata* 'Grandiflora')	Zones 3-8
Siberian weeping pea shrub (*Caranga arborescens* 'Pendula')	Zones 2-6
Variegated rockspray cotoneaster (*Cotoneaster atropurpureus* 'Variegatus')	Zones 4-7

"Plants most likely to survive severe weather in pots are drought-resistant broadleaved evergreens and conifers."

JUNE HUTSON

designs container plantings for the Missouri Botanical Garden in St. Louis and is a member of numerous gardening organizations.

Pair Plants *for* Eye-Catching *Containers*

(LEFT) Plants with similar needs grow well together. Treasure flower (*Gazania rigens*) and Dahlberg daisy (*Thymophylla tenuiloba*) both like dry conditions.

(INSET) Brightly colored and tropical plants look great around a pool. Sun coleus and datura appreciate the heat reflected from patio surfaces.

IT'S ALMOST TIME TO FILL those planters sitting out on your deck—but with what? While there's nothing wrong with standbys like impatiens, container gardens are a perfect opportunity to express your gardening style and exercise your creativity by combining several plants in a single pot.

Since most containers are planted to look good for just one season, there's no reason not to fill them up with unusual annuals, tender perennials, and tropical plants that will elicit a "Wow!" instead of a "Ho hum." Ornamental grasses can add dramatic textural contrast to plantings. And long-blooming, hardy perennials such as *Coreopsis verticillata* 'Moonbeam' or *Veronica* 'Sunny Border Blue' are also eye-catching alternatives.

CONSIDER DESIGN AND CULTURAL NEEDS

Container gardens are a great way to add a splash of color to the garden, so look for long-blooming plants and consider their care requirements. Most annuals will bloom all summer, but may need regular fertilization to keep them at their peak. Also, some annuals produce more flowers if they are deadheaded—the removal of faded flowers. Others are self-cleaning, meaning they shed their own spent flowers or keep blooming in spite of them. *Zinnia angustifolia*, periwinkle (*Catharanthus roseus*), and wax begonia (*Begonia* Semperflorens-Cultorum hybrids) are just a few that take care of themselves.

Leaf texture is as important as flower color, and the most interesting plant combinations feature leaves of contrasting texture. The spiky leaves of giant dracaena (*Cordyline*

Be adventurous with your choices. Lush umbrella tree (*Schefflera arboricola*) and Boston fern (*Nephrolepis exaltata* cvs.) are uncommon plants for outdoor containers.

"When creating container combinations, consider each plant's needs and grow like kinds together."

australis 'Atropurpurea') combined with the furry, gray foliage of *Salvia argentea* is stunning. Another striking combination is the ferny vervain (*Verbena* "Tapien Blue" and "Tapien Pink"), blooming in pink and purple, with the bold, mauve leaves of *Hibiscus acetosella*. Consider the broad foliage of caladium (*Caladium* × *hortulanum*) paired with filmy asparagus fern (*Asparagus filicinus*) for brightening shady corners.

The tallest plant in your container can either dominate the grouping or be blended into other, shorter flowers, but should not make the composition top-heavy. Plants that suit this purpose are canna (*Canna* × *generalis* hybrids), cosmos (*Cosmos bipinnatus*), rocket snapdragon (*Antirrhinum majus*) and, for large urns, tall verbena (*Verbena bonariensis*) or *Nicotiana sylvestris*. The width of the plant is not so important since plants are placed much closer together in a container than they are in the garden. A few leaves can be trimmed to keep the arrangement in bounds.

When creating container combinations, consider each plant's needs and grow like kinds together. Plants such as treasure flower (*Gazania rigens*), Dahlberg daisy (*Thymophylla tenuiloba*), and osteospermum (*Osteospermum* 'Sparkler' and other cvs.) prefer dry conditions and make handsome companions.

DEVELOP A PLANTING THEME

By identifying a theme, you can match container plantings to the style of your home or its surroundings. For a Victorian home, you might use an ornamental grass such as *Miscanthus sinensis* 'Cosmopolitan' as the focal point, surrounding it with a salmon-colored geranium (*Pelargonium* × *hortorum*), and cape leadwort (*Plumbago auriculata*).

Another choice for this theme combines the bold foliage and bicolored blossoms of butterfly flower (*Clerodendron ugandense*) with the ferny leaves of rose vervain (*Verbena canadensis* 'Candidissima') and the velvety flowers of 'Spring Blue' petunia.

For the cottage garden look, fill a container with bright flowers in varying forms and colors. A striking combination could feature the erect, annual tall verbena, whose poufs of purple flowers combine well with pink Egyptian star flower (*Pentas lanceolata* 'Starburst') and are set off by the steel-gray, ferny leaves of *Artemisia* 'Powis Castle'.

For a wilder arrangement in informal settings, try the burgundy-leaved, ornamental fountain grass (*Pennisetum setaceum* 'Rubrum') with the golden flowers of black-eyed Susan (*Rudbeckia hirta* 'Indian Summer'), and the trailing, frilly foliage and royal purple flowers of *Verbena* 'Imagination'.

A formal effect can be achieved by placing a rosemary (*Rosmarinus officinalis*) standard in a container and then surrounding it with sage (*Salvia officinalis*), thymes (*Thymus* spp.), or trailing, golden oregano (*Origanum vulgare* 'Aureum').

Miniature kitchen gardens can be created with a centerpiece of large herbs, such as lemon verbena (*Aloysia triphylla*) or pineapple sage (*Salvia elegans*). Basil cultivars (*Ocimum basilicum* 'Red Rubin' and 'Purple Ruffles') make great companions. Finish herb groupings with any of the mints (*Mentha* spp.) or trailing plants such as woolly thyme (*Thymus lanuginosus*).

For a poolside setting, use bright, bold colors to create a tropical feel in your mini-island retreat. Hibiscus (*Hibiscus rosa-sinensis*), both tall and shrubby, is happy in the summer heat. Surround it with green-and-white St. Augustine grass (*Stenotaphrum

secundatum* 'Variegatum') or the pure-blue flowers of *Evolvulus glomeratus* 'Blue Daze' for a hot summer combination. Contrast the salmon flowers of the cultivar 'Melissa' with trailing, black-leaved sweet potato vine (*Ipomoea batatas* 'Blackie'). Another combination with bright colors employs the red moss rose (*Portulaca grandiflora* 'Yubi Scarlet') and the chartreuse foliage of licorice plant (*Helichrysum petiolare* 'Limelight'). As a final suggestion, the vibrant leaf colors of the new sun coleus (*Solenostemon scutellarioides*) are great for giving the feel of a tropical setting.

A myriad of plant choices are at your fingertips to help create the specific look you want, so don't limit yourself. This year, dream up something really special for your container combinations.

Contrast leaf textures. The simple combination of dracaena and *Salvia argentea* is unforgettable.

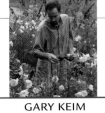

GARY KEIM

is a garden designer,
horticultural consultant,
writer, and editor.
Previously a designer at
Longwood Gardens,
he gardens near
Philadelphia.

Window Boxes
to Suit the Season

Summer blooms burst
from a sunny window
box at the author's
former home.

P ERFECT FOR AN APARTMENT dweller or
those with temporary living arrangements,
window boxes create garden opportunities
where there is no ground space. Window
boxes provide decoration to the often static
walls of our dwellings as well as add sparkle to our gardens. Their role has great appeal not only for gardeners
who have limited space but also those with established
gardens who are searching for venues in which to expand.

These elevated, self-contained gardens are fun to put
together, and are easily rearranged throughout the year to
reflect the spirit of each season.

As a professional gardener, I've grown plants in containers for years. I keep my own window boxes full of
flowers and greenery all the time. Here I'll give tips on
how to choose plants for window boxes, and how to plant
and maintain them.

SPRING: In perfect harmony, vibrant orange pansies and calendulas bloom among tufts of purple-flowering 'Crystal Palace' lobelia, while 'Gold Child' variegated ivy provides a trailing touch.

SELECTING THE PLANTS

Choosing plants for a window box shouldn't be a daunting experience. Your first impression may be an overwhelming myriad of choices, but if you set up parameters from a cultural as well as design point of view, the choices become easier. This will bring a focus to your planting scheme and ensure its survival. Match plants to the amount of sun the window box will receive while working within the bounds of a theme—perhaps a single color will dominate, or harmonious colors will play equal roles. Or concentrate solely on foliage. Use your imagination.

The window boxes at my previous home (which are pictured here) were located on a south-facing wall that received full sun all day. Naturally, this allowed a great variety of flowering plants to flourish. I also included in each seasonal scheme foliage plants—so important for providing contrast, cohesion, and background.

Window boxes in shade need not be flowerless; just choose shade-loving plants accordingly. However, you should pay particular attention to foliage in shady locations because the foliage plays a much more prominent role. Leaf size, texture, and color can be used for exciting effects.

I changed schemes four times during the garden season: spring, summer, autumn, and winter. (For seasonal planting schemes to fill a 4-foot-long box, see accompanying diagrams.) Due to the enormous root competition in a limited space, window-box plantings rarely stay in prime form throughout the season. Therefore, shorter seasonal displays are more appropriate. Occasionally, foliage

Spring Window Box

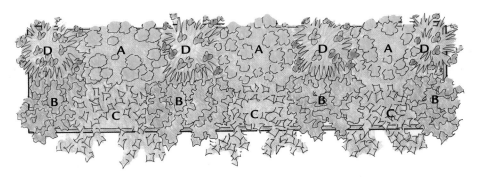

A. Pot marigold (*Calendula officinalis* 'Bon Bon Orange'), 3 plants
B. Lobelia (*Lobelia erinus* 'Crystal Palace'), 4–6 plants
C. English ivy (*Hedera helix* 'Gold Child'), 3 plants
D. Pansy (*Viola* × *wittrockiana* 'Padparadja'), 4–6 plants

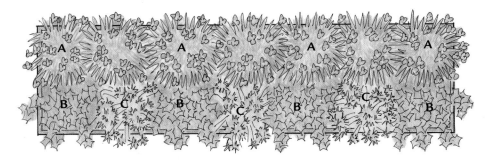

A. Pansy (*Viola* × *wittrockiana* 'Crystal Bowl Rose'), 6–7 plants
B. English ivy (*Hedera helix*), 4 plants
C. Swan river daisy (*Brachyscome* spp.), 3 plants

plants can be used again for another season's display. For instance, I kept ivies from the spring boxes and used them in the summer, autumn, and winter boxes. But flowering plants are usually spent and should be replaced after they've made their big splash.

When designing a planting scheme, pay particular attention to shapes of leaves and blossoms, using texture to provide visual interest. Also, take advantage of a plant's natural habit to flesh out a design. Ivies are perfect for trailing—visually breaking the edge of a box. Upright plants are best used near the rear, where they become accents. Finally,

plants with mounding or spreading habits are naturally suited for the middle section, rounding out the bulk of the window box. There are, of course, exceptions to these guidelines, and this makes for interesting design results. Experimentation usually brings exciting rewards.

Window-box displays rely on dense spacing to give voluptuous results. When planting, pay particular attention to placement, allowing enough room for each plant to develop while keeping plants slightly closer than if you were planting them in the garden.

SUMMER: A well-balanced design places tall plants at the back of a window box, mounding plants in the center and trailing plants at the front.

(INSET) Mahogany-leaved blood leaf combines with 'Orange Appeal' geranium and yellow-flowered *Bidens tenuifolia.*

"For me, the fine texture of ornamental grasses is the perfect complement to perennials and roses."

PLANTING THE WINDOW BOX

Window boxes can come in a variety of designs and be made of many different materials. They can be simple boxes, or can be gussied up with decorative trim. Wood, metal, and plastic boxes are most often encountered. Some are better than others.

Traditionally, window boxes are made of wood and painted; inevitably the boxes will need to be painted again and again. Metal boxes usually last several years before

rusting. And I've yet to find a plastic box I find appealing.

A much more attractive solution is to use window boxes made of a rot-resistant wood, such as cedar. Cedar holds up to moisture and will last for many years, gracefully aging and graying as time goes by.

After selecting a suitable window box, I begin filling it with the soil, or rather "growing medium," since the best medium for growing plants in window boxes is a soilless mix. (I use Pro-Mix.) These peat moss–based mixes are not only weed-free, fast-draining, and moisture retentive, they also are light-weight—a characteristic ideally suited to the suspended position of most window boxes.

While filling boxes with this mix, I like to add a slow-release, timed fertilizer like

Osmocote 14-14-14 and a water-absorbing polymer such as Hydrasorb, which is available at garden centers and from mail-order catalogs. The polymer particles expand when exposed to water, and create tiny "reservoirs" within the soilless mix. I've found this a great time-saver, as watering is greatly reduced when using these products.

Moisten the soil first, and soak the polymer crystals separately in a bucket so that they are expanded before you mix them into the soil. If they expand later, they may rise and overflow out of the window box.

Of course, watering is dependent on other factors. Use common sense to determine how frequently to water. Newly planted boxes may need watering only twice a week, while

Summer Window Box

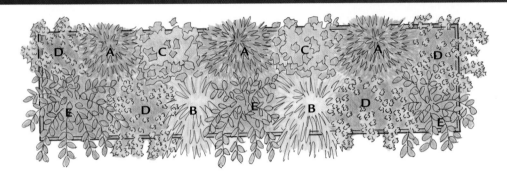

A. Blood leaf (*Iresine lindenii*), 3 plants
B. Asparagus fern (*Asparagus densiflorus*), 2 plants
C. Geranium (*Pelargonium* 'Orange Appeal'), 2 plants
D. Tickseed (*Bidens ferulifolia*), 4 plants
E. Greater periwinkle (*Vinca major* 'Aureo-variegata'), 3 plants

Alternate Summer Planting

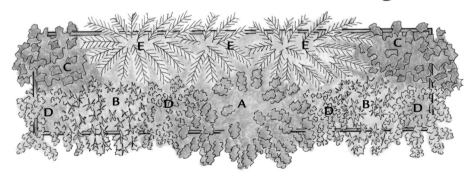

A. Rose Vervain (*Verbena canadensis* 'Homestead Purple'), 1 plant
B. Fairy fan flower (*Scaevola ameula* 'Blue Wonder'), 2 plants
C. Ivy geranium (*Pelargonium peltatum* 'Barock'), 2 plants
D. Variegated ground ivy (*Glechoma hederacea* 'Variegata'), 4 plants
E. Dusty miller (*Senecio viravira*), 3 plants

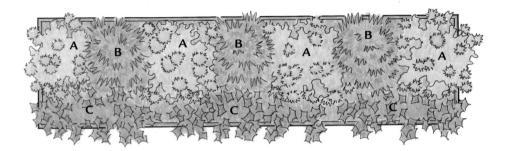

Autumn Window Box

A. *Chrysanthemum* spp., 4 plants
B. Hardy plumbago (*Ceratostigma plumbaginoides*), 3 plants
C. English ivy (*Hedera helix* 'Gold Child'), 3 plants

AUTUMN: Variegated English ivy mixes with bright yellow chrysanthemums and ruby-leaved hardy plumbago.

established ones may need watering once or twice a day in hot weather. Obviously, boxes in shade will remain moist longer than those in southern or very windy exposures. You can't count on rain to water your boxes, since they are often under house eaves where rain rarely falls.

Proper feeding is important because it helps to encourage healthy and vigorous foliage growth, which contributes to the tapestrylike effect of the planting. In addition to mixing slow-release fertilizer into the planting medium, it's mandatory to feed the plants regularly with a liquid fertilizer since soilless mixes are naturally low in fertility. I fertilize every two weeks at regular strength, and I know other gardeners who fertilize every week at half strength with equally fantastic results. I prefer Peter's 20-20-20. The important point is to remember to continue to feed the plants throughout the growing seasons.

Part of the wonder of window boxes is the beauty of having a flowering melange right at

Winter Window Box

A. English ivy (*Hedera helix*), 3 plants
B. Yew 'Hicksii' (*Taxus × media*), many branches
C. Winterberry (*Ilex verticillata*), many branches with red berries
D. Inkberry (*Ilex glabra*), many branches
E. Eastern white pine (*Pinus strobus*), many branches

WINTER: Red-berried hollies and boughs of yew and pine combine with last summer's ivy to brighten a snowy landscape.

eye level, but this high level of visibility also demands a higher level of maintenance. A daily routine is a small price to pay for the charm of a window box. Be diligent about removing spent blossoms, and marred and yellowing leaves. Pinch shoots regularly to keep plants compact and promote branching.

What better way to frame your outdoor views from inside than by giving them a flowery foreground in the form of a window box? Window boxes lend themselves both to spacious country gardens and space-starved city apartments. New compositions can supply a fresh, new look for every season.

LEE ANNE WHITE

is consulting editor
and former chief editor
of *Fine Gardening*, a
Master Gardener, and a
professional garden
photographer.

Focus on Foliage

for a Soothing Setting

Combine potted plants
with varying forms.
The strong vertical or
fountainlike forms of
ornamental grasses go
well with mounding,
sprawling, and trailing
plants.

I'VE ALWAYS LOVED REARRANGING furniture. When I was first setting up house, I'd get home from work, kick off my heels, and start shoving sofas around. These days, however, I prefer pushing my pots about. They're all filled with foliage plants, and I love experimenting with different combinations of leaf texture, color, and form.

TEXTURE PLAYS A KEY ROLE

Usually when people think about container plantings, they picture colorful pots of flowering annuals. My deck gets only a few hours of sun each day, so I opt primarily for plants with great foliage. To keep the plants from looking alike, I pay attention to their leaf texture (whether glossy, rough, fuzzy, or prickly) and form (which runs the gamut from mounded and fountainlike to trailing and spiky). By contrasting these features, you can create a surprising amount of visual interest without flowers.

fuzzy leaves of *Plectranthus*, the rubbery foliage of *Canna*, and the prickly spikes of blue fescue (*Festuca glauca*). But there's also visual texture: Just imagine the filigreed foliage of maidenhair fern (*Adiantum pedatum*) against the bold, puckered leaves of a giant blue hosta (*Hosta sieboldiana*).

RELY ON JAZZY LEAF COLOR

While green is the most common leaf color, there are many great plants with striking foliage colors—such as coleus (*Solenostemon scutellarioides*), sweet potato vines (*Ipomoea batatas* 'Blackie' and 'Marguerite'), *Canna* hybrids, bananas (*Musa* spp.), golden sedges (*Carex* spp.), and even many shrubs. I'm a sucker for almost any plant with gold, burgundy, or blue foliage. They look great with green and with each other. Favorites include Bowles' golden sedge (*Carex elata* 'Aurea'), purple fountain grass (*Pennisetum setaceum* 'Rubrum'), and blue fescue (*Festuca glauca*). There are even sedges with brown foliage, like *Carex buchananii*.

But even with green, you have a lot of choices. The glossy-green, serrated leaves of germander (*Teucrium chamaedrys*) contrast dramatically with the bright chartreuse foliage of golden creeping Jenny (*Lysimachia nummularia* 'Aurea'). And some foliage is more gray-green, like the variegated grape-leaf begonia (*Begonia* 'Magic Lace').

Variegated foliage, especially when rimmed in white, brightens my container combinations. Variegated *Plectranthus forsteri* 'Marginatus' is striking against the dark, strappy foliage of New Zealand flax (*Phormium tenax*). Silver foliage is also an eyeopener, and *Artemisia* species and cultivars offer many choices. As with texture and form, go for contrast in colors, pairing bright and dark shades for best effect.

Contrast leaf shape and color. The gray-green, palmate leaves of plume poppy (*Macleaya cordata*) are striking with the chartreuse, heart-shaped leaves of sweet potato vine (*Ipomoea batatas* 'Marguerite') and the colorful, serrated foliage of a coleus.

A good example is the sprawling, finely textured, and hairy-stemmed Australian tree fern (*Cyathea cooperi*) I use as a backdrop to the bold leaves of elephant ears (*Colocasia* spp.) and the slender, arching blades of fountain grass (*Pennisetum alopecuroides* 'Little Bunny'). Although their shapes and textures contrast, the overall effect is soothing.

There are two ways to look at texture. The first has to do with how foliage feels: the

Variegation is eye-catching. The white edges of this *Salvia nipponica* 'Fuji Snow' stand out in this scene, even though it's the smallest plant in the arrangement.

Ornamental grasses
provide subtle color
and strong shapes.

Combine plants
with contrasting leaf
texture.

Group pots closely
together to create
a garden unto
themselves.

USE A FEW
FLOWERS FOR ACCENT

Most container gardeners focus on flowers, but I use flowers only as occasional accents. Call me crazy but I often rush to remove flowers from my container plants as soon as they appear. My angel-wing begonias, for instance, are rarely permitted to bloom in this garden. And while it would be contrary to nature's ways, I'd be perfectly happy if my cannas never flowered; it's the colorful, striped foliage of *Canna* 'Pretoria' and 'Tropicanna' that I love most.

Even though flowers aren't the stars of the show, they do accent my container plantings. I prefer those with subtle colors, like the maroon flowers of Joe Pye weed (*Eupatorium maculatum*) and the silvery inflorescences of *Miscanthus sinensis*. In fact, most of the flowers in my container garden are those of ornamental grasses. Their earthy colors blend right in, and I love the way they sway in the slightest breeze.

Fragrance is also a determining factor. Valerian (*Valeriana officinalis*), which I originally planted for its lovely pinnate leaves, delighted me with the heady fragrance of its white flowers, so it stays.

REDUCED MAINTENANCE
IS A PLUS

Although it wasn't my goal, I've found that maintaining containers with foliage plants is easier than keeping up colorful pots of flowers. There are fewer fading flowers to deadhead, and foliage needs only occasional sprucing up. And instead of fertilizing weekly, I just mix in a pelletized, slow-release fertilizer

"I'm a sucker for almost any plant with gold, burgundy, or blue foliage. They look great with green and with each other."

at planting time and then give my plants a drink of liquid fertilizer two or three times over the summer.

Because my containers are mostly in shade, I don't have to water quite as often, either. In a sunny setting, I might water daily. With my shady foliage garden, watering every two or three days is usually sufficient.

ARRANGE AND REARRANGE

Whether you place a single plant or group of plants in a pot, you can create an entire garden of potted foliage plants. Simply pack the pots in close together, rearranging for just the right effect. I'll place some pots in the back on supports for greater height and let plants with trailing foliage sit up front. If you work at it, you can even give the impression there aren't any pots. Of course, I love interesting pots, too, and often use them as focal points, working to coordinate the colors of the pots and the foliage.

I find that as plants grow throughout the season, I'm given new opportunities for creating interesting arrangements. But even if you're not into rearranging your pots at the end of the work day, take a fresh look at foliage plants the next time you visit the nursery and pick up a few for your own container garden. You'll discover that the overall effect is very soothing.

WESLEY ROUSE

is a landscape designer and the owner of Pine Meadow Gardens, a nursery and landscaping service in Southbury, Connecticut.

Three-Season
Container
Plantings

This summer container is filled with tender tropicals, like *Canna* 'Tropicana', coleus, and the trailing sweet potato vine *(Ipomoea batatas* 'Marguerite') for a bold splash of color.

I N MANY PARTS OF THE COUNTRY, outdoor containers are underutilized. They hold a few annuals from the last frost until summer's end, then sit empty for the rest of the year. Yet with a little effort, it's possible to extend a container's interest by several weeks at each end of the growing season. The key is to plant a container not once, but twice or even three times, changing the plants with the seasons to create a beautiful, living arrangement that lasts from early spring well into fall.

In my garden here in western Connecticut, I plant my containers three times during the growing season—once in early spring (usually the middle of March), a second time after the last frost date for this area (mid- to late May) and a third time in late summer (about the middle of September). By taking advantage of spring and fall, I add three months of interest to the usual frost-free growing season. As a result, I have attractive containers by my

How to Plant in Containers

1. Fill the container to about 80 percent capacity with moistened soilless mix.

2. Before planting, break up plant root balls to encourage roots to branch out into the soil mix.

front door, on my terrace, and in my gardens featuring a variety of plants from pansies to mums.

This technique does take some extra effort. You'll need to spend a modest amount of time buying new plants, but it takes only minutes to replant a container. The pleasure of beautiful flowers and foliage is well worth the trouble. I replant several of the containers around the house and gardens to change with the season, and my staff replants con-

> *"By replanting a container as the seasons change, you can have flowers from early spring to hard autumn frosts."*

tainers for many of my landscaping clients. Once you begin planting seasonal containers, you'll wonder why you put up with such long winters.

COLD-TOLERANT PLANTS EXTEND THE SEASON

Extending the season in a container means choosing plants that don't flinch in the face of cold weather. Pansies (*Viola* × *wittrockiana*) and Iceland poppies (*Papaver croceum*) are standards of spring; chrysanthemums and ornamental cabbages and kales (*Brassica oleracea*) are fall classics. But there are other plants, both annuals and perennials, that thrive in cool temperatures—enough to make striking container arrangements

3. Plant closely so the container arrangement looks finished as soon as it's planted.

4. After planting, add more soil mix to bring the level to within an inch or two of the rim.

5. Finally, water with a dilute mix of water-soluble fertilizer.

despite the threat of frost. You may find a fair selection of cold-tolerant plants at your local garden center. Talk with fellow gardeners and consult books to learn about plants that aren't commonly available in your area but that you can order by mail. I supplement the selection of plants I can buy by starting some plants from seeds, and I overwinter others from cuttings.

PLANT CLOSELY FOR A STRONG IMMEDIATE IMPRESSION

Planting a container is an easy gardening project. Once you've assembled the basic ingredients—a container with one or more drainage holes in the bottom, soil mix, and plants—you can finish the job in minutes.

The first step is to fill the container with a fluffy, fast-draining soil mix. I use a commercial peat moss–based soilless mix because, unlike garden soil, it is lightweight and fast-draining. But the peat moss is slow to absorb moisture, so if you use a soilless mix, you must moisten it—adding water and stirring it with your hand until it's damp, not soggy—in a tub or a bucket before adding it to the container. Then fill the container about 80 percent full with damp mix, allowing room for the root balls of the plants, which can displace a fair amount of mix.

Before planting, set the plants—still in their pots—inside the container to see if you like the effect. When you're pleased with your arrangement, start planting. Work from

the center of the container to the edges. Pause to break up the root balls with your fingers as you plant. Breaking up the root ball damages roots slightly, encouraging the plant to produce new, lateral roots that will grow into the surrounding soil mix. If the root ball is left undisturbed, the roots may not grow out of the shape of the nursery pot, stunting the plant's growth.

When you plant, plant closely. You want the container to look finished as soon as you've planted it. That said, you do need to leave some room for growth. Experience will teach you how much growth to expect from a given plant in a season.

The author's early spring container includes (FROM TOP TO BOTTOM) white marguerite daisies; pink and white Iceland poppies; blue forget-me-nots; the variegated, sword-shaped leaves of an iris relative named *Neomarica*; pink snapdragons; and the white flowers of a trailing moss verbena. This colorful arrangement brightened the steps leading to the author's front door for several weeks before the danger of frost had passed.

Spring

PLANTING DIAGRAM

Upright form
1. Marguerite (*Leucanthemum vulgare*)
2. *Neomarica gracilis*
3. Iceland poppy (*Papaver croceum*)

Rounded form
4. Forget-me-not
   (*Myosotis sylvatica* 'Ultramarine')
5. Dwarf pink snapdragon
   (*Antirrhinum* 'Silk Pink')

Trailing form
6. Moss verbena
   (*Verbena tenuisecta* 'Alba')

ALTERNATIVE PLANTS
Upright form
* Spring bulbs, such as daffodils
  (*Narcissus* spp.) or tulips (*Tulipa* spp.)
* Leopard's bane (*Doronicum orientale*)

Rounded form
* Primroses (*Primula* spp.)
* Bleeding heart (*Dicentra* spp.)
* Stock (*Matthiola incana*)

Trailing form
* Greater periwinkle (*Vinca major*)

With the garden as backdrop, the author's summer container overflows with (from top to bottom) red fountain grass, rose-pink pentas, the black leaves of a black sweet potato, the silver leaves of the licorice plant, and the purple-throated, white flowers of cup flower.

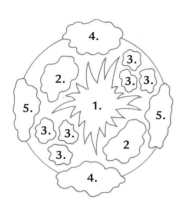

PLANTING DIAGRAM

Upright form
1. Red fountain grass
(*Pennisetum setaceum* 'Rubrum')

Rounded form
2. Egyptian star cluster, rose-pink
form (*Pentas lanceolata*)

Trailing form
3. White cup (*Nierembergia repens*)
4. Licorice plant (*Helichrysum petiolare*)
5. Black sweet potato
(*Ipomoea batatas* 'Blackie')

ALTERNATIVE PLANTS
Upright form
- Dwarf ornamental grasses
(e.g. *Miscanthus* spp. and *Pennisetum*
spp.)

Rounded form
- Small-flowered petunia (*Petunia* spp.)
- Annual geranium (*Pelargonium* spp.)
- Madagascar periwinkle
(*Catharanthus roseus*)

Trailing form
- Swan river daisy (*Brachyscome iberidifolia*)
- Lamb's ears (*Stachys byzantina*)
- Bugelweed (*Ajuga* spp.)

After planting, add more soil mix, if necessary, to bring the soil level to within an inch or two of the top of the container. Then water your new arrangement thoroughly (until water runs out the drainage hole) with a dilute mix of water-soluble 20-20-20 fertilizer.

Your container is now off to a good start, but it won't reach its potential without regular care. Water the container by hand whenever the soil mix feels dry (don't rely on rain or sprinkler systems, which rarely moisten more than the top few inches of mix). Fertilize the plants in the container regularly—either with a full-strength mix of water-soluble fertilizer on a weekly basis, or with a dilute mix every time you water. The fertilizer replaces nutrients that are washed out of the container when you water. Also, remove spent flowers to encourage strong growth and continued heavy flowering.

EVALUATE YOUR POTS AT SEASON'S END

Replanting a container at the end of a season is simple. Once you've gathered together the plants you want to include for the next season's display, empty the container of plants. Scoop them out with a trowel or tip the container onto its side to pull out plants that have grown into a tightly woven mass. Replace lost soil mix. Then re-set plants from the preceding season that you want to keep in the container and add new ones.

Which plants stay and which go depends on their adaptability to changing growing conditions. Some cold-tolerant plants—verbenas, for example—can flower from earliest spring, through summer and into fall. You can leave such plants in a container all season long. Other cold-tolerant plants bloom for a shorter period or stop blooming with the onset of warm weather, at which time they should be removed. You can transplant the perennials among them into the garden for years of future enjoyment.

Undeterred by early autumn frosts, the plants in the author's fall container—which includes a pink chrysanthemum; the blue and purple, sculpted leaves of ornamental kales; white pansies; and the grasslike leaves of a variegated lilyturf—add a spark of color to a stone walk.

Fall

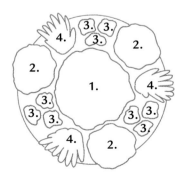

PLANTING DIAGRAM

Upright form
1. Pink-flowered mum
   (*Chrysanthemum* spp.)

Rounded form
2. Ornamental kale
   (*Brassica oleracea* 'Frizzy Red')
3. White pansies (*Viola × wittrockiana* 'Crystal Bowl White')

Trailing form
4. Variegated lilyturf (*Liriope muscari* 'Silver Dragon')

ALTERNATIVE PLANTS
Upright form
- Ornamental sages (e.g. *Salvia greggii*)
- Fall-blooming asters (*Aster* spp.)

Rounded form
- Lady's mantle (*Alchemilla* spp.)
- Plumbago
  (*Ceratostigma plumbaginoides*)

Trailing form
- Greater periwinkle (*Vinca major*)
- Moss verbena (*Verbena tenuisecta*)

SELECTING
CONTAINERS

3

WHILE THE MOST BASIC FUNCTION of a container is to hold plants, it also serves as an accent in the garden. Just the right pot in just the right place can make a world of difference. Whether your tastes run toward traditional or eclectic, the possibilities are endless. Terra-cotta pots have been a favorite for hundreds of years and for good reason, but there are many other wonderful choices available—from window boxes and hanging baskets, to wooden planters and whiskey barrels, to lightweight, synthetic containers and recycled housewares. Your choice of container is limited only by your imagination. Some pots do require special care. Terra-cotta pots, for instance, should be brought indoors before cold winter weather sets in. And cleaning containers regularly helps prevent disease and the buildup of mineral deposits. We'll show you how to clean and care for your pots with a minimum of effort.

Terra-cotta pots—the all-time favorite—come in all shapes and sizes, and from plain to decorative styles.

Lots *of* Pots

MELISSA MCLAUGHLIN

is the owner of Country Garden Nursery in McMinnville, Oregon, a family-run nursery specializing in large hanging flower baskets.

THE WELL PLACED CONTAINER can make all the difference in the attitude of a garden. On my first visit to Butchart Gardens in Victoria, British Columbia, my eyes were drawn to the pots, not the plants. Most people remember the flowers, but I was visiting in January. The reflecting pool in the Italian plaza lay dormant, kept company only by the silent sentinels of large, stone urns, waiting patiently for spring's arrival. Their sides festooned with acanthus leaves, the urns quietly evoked the hope of warmer days. Planted with small cypress trees, they lent structure and balance to a courtyard that might otherwise have looked forgotten.

CHOOSE POTS FOR THEIR APPEAL

At the most basic level, all containers allow us to plant where there is no earth: on flagstone patios, redwood terraces, the sides of buildings, street-side lampposts, or

"At the most basic level, all containers allow us to plant where there is no earth."

Pay Attention to Weight

A 24-inch container full of soil mix may easily outweigh most gardeners. Wheeled dollies make larger pots more movable. However, a filled half barrel is about their maximum load. If your container is going to hang, consider what it may weigh when full of soil and plants dripping wet. The 24-inch-diameter baskets that I plant for my commercial clients tip the scales at 150 pounds plus—a bit much for the average suburban front porch.

high-rise balconies. But containers also add decorative accents to gardens. Used like sculpture, they can give flavor or focus to a setting. They also bring the beauty of plants closer, making it more accessible to the city dweller or the elderly.

As a nursery owner and gardener in Oregon, the containers I use most often are wire baskets that completely disappear under their bounty of flowers. Most garden centers sell terra-cotta or plastic pots in dozens of shapes and sizes, as well as wooden and stone planters and lightweight containers made of synthetic materials. You can also use almost any container you find, from castoff shoes to old pots and sinks to flat tires. Only your imagination limits what you can use for a container. Look in antiques shops, hardware

stores, even your own backyard. If you can make it hold soil, you can grow plants in it. Even a dead tree or a rock with a fissure in it can be used as a container. Most solid materials can be drilled for drainage or, if they are too porous (such as baskets), lined with cocoa fiber for water and soil retention.

Design considerations aside, I look for durability when purchasing containers. Will it hold up to bumping by chairs, dogs, or kids on the patio? Will it be used year-round in a climate that freezes? Basketry is cute, but simply won't hold up for more than a season of annuals. A tiered set of metal produce baskets on the other hand, will need to be lined to hold in the soil, but will last long enough to use for small perennials that can survive the winter.

Terra-cotta is one of the best materials for containers because it is porous, letting roots breathe. Its drawbacks are its heavy weight relative to plastic or fiberglass and its breakability. Its looks improve with age, gaining a greenish mossy tint.

High-fired terra-cotta, which generally comes from Italy and England, is fairly durable. You can tell a high-fired pot by its smooth surface, the heavy weight, and the clear "ping" when you tap its side. Italian pottery, in particular, is known for its dense quality and ability to hold up through the seasons.

Much of Mexico's pottery is low-fired and not designed for harsh winters. Low-fired pots tend to have a thick, rough surface and are lightweight. Water will seep into the pores and upon freezing, the clay flakes off in layers or the entire pot cracks. Decorated terra-cotta pots from Asia and the South Pacific have a rustic beauty, but they can be too porous to survive for long in a cold climate. I have successfully weatherproofed an "iffy" clay pot from Asia by painting tar on the inside and clear sealer on the outside.

"Only your imagination limits what you can use for a container."

THINK BEYOND TERRA-COTTA

Some containers call to us from centuries past. Great square wooden citrus boxes with globes on each top corner were built for Louis XIV's garden at Versailles. These were painted to prevent rot, and designed to open on all sides like a magician's box, enabling the gardener to prune the roots. Wooden boxes should be made of a naturally rot-resistant wood such as cedar or redwood. Paint is fine, but don't use pressure-treated wood; it can leach toxic chemicals into the soil.

Lead and copper urns probably show up more in European gardens, but if you are lucky enough to find one in an antiques shop, go for it. With proper drainage, you'll have a long-lasting piece that will only improve as the patina of age mellows it. It's best to limit metal containers to shady spots,

Select pots with personality. Terra-cotta, ceramic, wood, metal, and stone containers come in all shapes and sizes. But don't stop there—if it's something that can hold soil, you can plant in it.

ground plantings, and the smaller the pot, the faster it will dry out. A 15-inch or bigger pot will do well with once-a-day watering in my summers.

SHAPE AND STYLE MATTER

The shape of the container and the kinds of plants are also important. An urn with a narrow neck has less surface for planting, but may be very nice for a single plant, such as a clump of variegated yucca. But when the plant needs repotting as it grows larger, will you be able to remove it without breaking the pot or destroying the plant? Sometimes this can be avoided by placing a plastic pot with your plant inside the more decorative one. It should be raised inside on a chunk of brick to ensure drainage and the right height.

The style of the containers you choose is of utmost importance. A well-chosen container will enhance your entry, patio, or grotto for years. Do consider the architecture of your house, especially the details. These are the clues to echo in the containers, for they are structural components that link the house and garden. Is the woodwork natural or painted? Is the concrete finish smooth or textured? Terra-cotta does not enhance all types of architecture but looks great with brick, stucco, and adobe.

Color in glaze, paint, or plastic is limitless. Choose thoughtfully. It is easier to change plants than the color of your container. Some gardeners like to use a neutral pot color to allow plants to speak for themselves.

Whether your garden is a formal planting of ivy and evergreens or an eclectic mix born of your insatiable plant collecting, the right containers will enhance that style. Subtle or eye-catching, containers will give dimension and personality to your own patch of Eden.

since metal can become very hot in the sun and cook the roots of your plants.

Cement pots offer a surprising range of style variations from ancient to modern. They are almost indestructible, but they do chip, and this can be unsightly. Hypertufa is a related material made from peat moss, sand, and Portland cement. It is usually used to form a rustic-looking trough that is popular for alpine collections.

New on the market is a hard foam material called Thermo-Lite. Cast into Italian-style molds and painted to look like hefty cement or clay pots, these containers are fabulous. They hold up to quite a bit of abuse and look amazingly like the real thing, but weigh almost nothing. They cost no more than terra-cotta pots of similar size.

The size of your container should be in scale with its surroundings. Pots always seem to shrink in the space between the store shelf and the outdoor site, so I have trained myself to select a larger pot than I think I need. I don't like to use anything smaller than 15 inches in diameter. I plant pots to look full immediately, and I can't fit an assortment of plants into anything less than 15 inches. A more practical reason is watering. Containers all dry out much faster than in-

Cleaning and Disinfecting Pots

Pots can be reused, but they accumulate mineral deposits and other debris inside and out that can harbor disease. So for the plant's sake, you should clean and disinfect your pots each time you plant in them.

Mineral salts can be unsightly and can damage plants. Minerals, which are dissolved in water, leach through the walls of clay pots, forming a white film on them. They can also accumulate around the rims of both clay and plastic pots.

This white, crusty film is merely unsightly when deposited on pot walls, but when it encrusts the rim of a pot, the mineral salts can dehydrate plant stems that rest there.

—Delilah Smittle

First, disinfect, then scrub used pots. To disinfect clay pots, soak them in a solution of 1 part household bleach to 9 parts water for 10 minutes or more. Next, dip them into a solution of water and dish detergent.

Lift the pots from the soapy water and scrub away as much dirt and mineral deposits as you can using steel wool or a wire-bristle brush. Scrape any remaining mineral deposits from the walls and the rim of the pot with a knife. When pots are clean, rinse them off and soak them in clean water until you are ready to use them. (Dry clay pots can wick moisture from the potting medium, dehydrating newly potted plants.)

Plastic pots can be disinfected and cleaned in the same way as clay pots, except that you can easily remove salts and debris with a scouring pad. If any mineral salts cling to the rim of a plastic pot after it's been scrubbed, simply scrape them off with a knife and smooth the pot edges with steel wool. Rinse the pot clean, and it's ready to use.

J-P MALOCSAY, a professional gardener and writer in Landenberg, Pennsylvania, conducts workshops on container gardening and rustic twigwork.

New Life *for* Old Housewares

A blue kettle complements plants in shades of white and green. Variegated Solomon's seal (*Polygonatum odoratum* 'Variegatum') arches above *Viola tricolor* 'Princess Cream'.

I HAVE THIS SHADOWY CHILDHOOD memory of a battered dishpan glowing with *Portulaca grandiflora* in the hot summer light. An old woman is calling it "moss rose." This fragment of early delight may account for the abiding love I have for growing things in old-time housewares.

My favorite castaway planters are old enamelwares that did many of the jobs now done by plastics. Lightweight metal enamelware didn't break when banged and didn't rust until repeated hits chipped the porcelain finish. No wonder stoves and washing machines still feature this user-friendly surface.

USE PIECES PAST THEIR PRIME OR AFFORDABLE NEW ONES

Most of my enamel kettles and such wore out on the job donkey's years before I met up with them. Some were gifts from old folks. Others were flea-market and country-

Group housewares to contrast colors, shapes, and sizes. This trio stars a canning pot with stinking hellebore (*Helleborus foetidus*). Its companions contain two types of mondo grass (*Ophiopogon* spp.).

supply, and camping stores. The same goes for other tin and galvanized wares of bygone days. Galvanized buckets and tubs come in many shapes, some downright graceful. Look to them for container gardening on a larger scale—cannas reaching for the sky.

I mostly use housewares in sizes from canners—those big pots used for canning produce—on down. My wickedly thorny 'Flying Dragon' bitter orange (*Poncirus trifoliata* 'Flying Dragon') is 3 feet tall after four years in its canner. It could just as well be one of the many gorgeously sculptural *Chamaecyparis* that I've yearned to contain for years on end, and someday will.

My favorite large enamelware is a low, wide kettle for simmering tomato sauce. It looks good with plants that grow low or high—from hostas to tree peonies to vines climbing a trellis or scrambling overboard.

Sometimes my old containers just sit around till the right plant notion comes along. When a coffeepot and mixing bowl—both enamel—proved too hard for boring holes, I thought of floating aquatics. The rounded leaves of water pennywort (*Hydrocotyle verticillata*) looked just right in the rotund coffeepot. Water hyacinth (*Eichhornia crassipes*) filled the mixing bowl and even bloomed on a winter windowsill.

One year my black enamel skillet simmered with delicate fairy moss (*Azolla caroliniana*). Now it holds just one of many possible bog or waterside miniatures—a tiny, chartreuse cultivar of *Acorus gramineus* fanning around a rock.

dump finds. Many led such full lives that they came to me leaking like sieves. Fortunately, the rust holes provide necessary drainage. I cover them with a mesh screen to keep the soil from spilling out. In others, I make quarter-inch holes every few inches, using a hammer and a nailset. The trick is to rest the metal to be pierced on a block of wood. This takes the dent out of banging, and minimizes the flaking (and later rusting) of enamel finishes.

I never punch holes in collector wares or even old pieces still fit for use. There's plenty of throwaway stuff to garden with. There's even new to buy, since enamelware is making a modest comeback in hardware, home-

MOVE CONTAINERS AROUND UNTIL THEY FEEL AT HOME

Like all garden oddments, old housewares need to be used well and in moderation. One way to deal with oddities is to group them as

a collection, as with family pictures. Another way is to let the odd piece blend into a context, like the family dog in a family picture.

I tend to move my planted housewares around the garden, trying out various contexts. A few come inside for winter, or for days at a time in spring, when bad weather keeps me in. Imagine savoring a kettle full of blooming bearded iris safe at hand while rain and wind tatter all outdoors. The modest-sized iris I grow is in scale with its low, wide kettle.

Its long time in leaf is satisfying too. The fans set up a quiet harmony of green with its companion myrtle spurge (*Euphorbia myrsinites*) even as their postures contrast.

The spurge blooms in May, then adds fresh green for the duration. As summer comes on, fleabane (*Erigeron karvinskianus*) adds its airy cloud of tiny daisies till frost. That kettle joins others in sheltered ground over winter. A kettle planted with hardy *Sedum* or *Sempervivum* can sit aboveground year-round—adjusting for winter exposure. Succulent plants are perfect for these house-

Let old housewares suggest new uses in the garden. A black enamel skillet is lush with a chartreuse cultivar of *Acorus gramineus* surrounding a rock.

"Like all garden oddments, old housewares need to be used well and in moderation."

wares. They have that look of steady purpose, like good, solid food.

Some containers have busy surfaces, like old-time "agateware." Its enamel finish splashes white and blue together, quirky and restless. A succulent with sculptural mass and simple lines will slow it down. Or you can fight jazz with jazz, filling agateware with energetic plants such as those with silver, variegated, or finely divided foliage. Add a tireless bloomer around the rim and you get a hyperactive composition.

USE CONTAINER PLANTINGS TO SET A MOOD

Whatever I do, I like containers to look at home. So much depends on how you live. I'm writing this in June. The kitchen door stands open. The garden crowds the porch, and the porch is crowded with plants. I'm struck by the air of calm in these containers close to the house. True, down by the barn there's that razzle-dazzle agateware. But here, just outside the door, I look at peaceful, largely perennial combinations in these homey old wares. Some unnamed golden hosta shares its black kettle with bright-gold ivy spilling over one way. *Begonia sutherlandii* leans out the other way with oddly radiant, green-gold leaves and single, orange flowers with bright yellow anthers. I see this container as bright, but sedate, definitely grown-up. No blazing dishpan of moss rose here, no siree. Where has that half century gone anyway?

Time is of the essence when gardeners design, and containers certainly focus our attention. Here, in this one small space, we hope to manage whole lives of plants. Maybe whole human lives too, if we stop to think about planting to please something in ourselves.

(ABOVE) Move containers around till they seem at home. A black kettle holding a 'Shima Daijin' tree peony perches where it's reflected in a half-barrel pond.

(RIGHT) Play off the color of a recycled container. A rusty boiler inspired this planting of *Cordyline australis* 'Atrosanguinea', *Phormium tenax*, *Pelargonium* 'Vancouver Centennial', *Lysimachia nummularia* 'Aurea', and a dwarf orange *Celosia argentea*.

KATE HUNTER

has been gardening in her
small garden in Urbana,
Illinois, for more than
20 years. Her passion for
terra-cotta inspired her
to create her first Tudor
willow cage.

A Hoop Trellis for Containers

In English gardens, hoop trellises are traditionally planted with carnations, but many other plants, such as lavender, work equally well.

I T'S HARD TO BE AN ADMIRER of English gardens in Central Illinois. I'd love to turn my backyard into one of those gardens you see in the pages of British gardening books. But England doesn't have the extremes of weather we have here—cold, dry, bitter winters and hot, stressful summers.

While I may not be able to grow the same plants as English gardeners, I have found something from England that translates well to my garden. I've figured out how to make the beautiful hoop trellises made of willow branches that were used in Tudor knot gardens to provide support for tall plants. When these willow cages are set in terra-cotta pots and planted with colorful flowers, they provide a focal point all season long in my packed and busy borders. A cage takes about two hours to make, and all the materials are fairly easy to come by.

Pencil-thick willow switches make up the hoops. You'll need two 42 inches long, four 36 inches long, and four 26 inches long.

A SQUAT POT, SWITCHES, AND A FEW OTHER SUPPLIES

I think the cage looks best when it is a bit taller than the pot it sits in. The measurements given here are for a pot with a diameter of 11 inches. I recommend using a terracotta azalea pot, which is wider than it is tall. It also has nearly vertical walls, which help the cage sit in it snugly.

Willow switches, or rods, as basket makers call them, are ideal for the cage since they are very supple. Any willow (*Salix* spp.) with straight branches will do. You will need green shoots, which you can cut at any time of the year. If you can't find a willow tree, you can use tender shoots from apple, pear, or other hardwood trees instead. Keep your eye out for stumps because they'll often sprout straight new shoots.

You'll need 10 long, uniformly thick switches approximately the diameter of a pencil (¼ inch) for the hoops. You may have to search the tree to find switches that are

long enough. If you can, cut about twenty 4-foot lengths to ensure that you have a good supply. Cut an additional 20 to 25 switches somewhat smaller in diameter for weaving. You'll also need a flexible tape measure, a hand pruner to trim the switches, a pail of warm water to soak the switches in, and plastic-coated wire twist ties to hold the cage together while you work. And you'll need heavy thread with some tooth to it to tie the parts of the cage together; old-fashioned carpet or button thread works best. If you don't have a spool stowed away in a sewing basket, you can find one at a sewing store.

When you're ready to make the cage, peel the leaves and snip off the side branches from the willow switches. Cut the two best-looking thick switches 42 inches long for the main hoops. Cut four thick switches 36 inches long for the middle hoops, and four more 26 inches long for the lower hoops. Lightly mark these switches at their midpoint and place

1. Place the two main hoops (color-coded purple) first. Secure with tape and a twist tie.

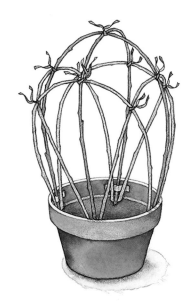

2. Add the four middle hoops (green). Hold in place with twist ties.

3. Add the four lower hoops (red).

4. Weave a 1½-inch band of thin switches above the pot rim.

5. Tie knots with heavy thread to replace the twist ties.

the switches in a deep pail of water. They can be used in about a week.

START IN THE CENTER AND WORK DOWN

To help you position the hoops in the pot, lightly mark the inside rim of the pot at the 12 o'clock position, and again at 3, 6, and 9 o'clock. Put the two main hoops inside the pot at right angles to each other so that each end extends 3 inches into the pot, and so that the branches line up with your quarter marks (see sidebar step 1). Use a twist tie to hold the marked centers together. You may wish to temporarily tape the ends to the inside of the pot to prevent them from popping out.

Then curve one of the middle hoops, and place the ends on each side of one of the main hoops. The top of the curve should rest about a third of the way down outside the main hoop (see sidebar step 2). Turn the pot 180 degrees and place the second hoop the same way. Turn 90 degrees and repeat for the third and fourth hoops. Using twist ties, fasten the middle hoops to the main hoops at the points of intersection.

The lower hoops are placed in the same way, but the tops of their curves intercept the main hoops about two thirds of the way down (see sidebar step 3). To make the cage more stable, weave the lower hoops in front of and behind the middle and main hoops

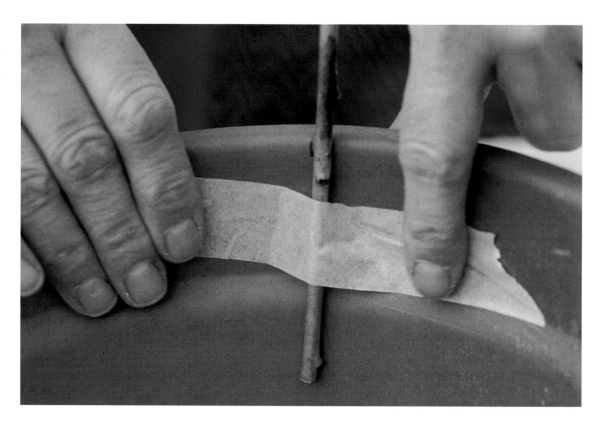

It helps to anchor the two main hoops to the pot with masking tape.

where you can. Fasten the remaining intersections with twist ties, using the center points marked on each hoop to guide you.

Then take a few minutes to view the cage from all sides. Loosen the ties and adjust the hoops to balance the shape and refine the symmetry.

HOLDING THE HOOPS IN PLACE

The next step is to secure the hoops by weaving in the thinner willow switches. Keeping one hand to the inside of the cage and one to the outside, weave the soaked willow in an over-and-under pattern around all the hoops right above the pot rim (see sidebar step 4 on p. 93). I find it's easiest to stick the switch in to its midpoint, then weave out in both directions.

Start new switches at different places along the rim so that the ends are not all on the same side. Make sure successive rows alternate to create a woven effect. If a switch breaks, just push the broken end to the inside and clip off the extra. After weaving two layers, make final adjustments to the hoop placement. Weave as many layers as you like. I recommend a minimum of six—a width of about 1½ inches. Keep the layers pushed down tight against the rim and against each other.

I like to tie the hoops together where they intersect so that the cage will stay neat and formal-looking (see sidebar step 5 on p. 93). You don't have to tie them together, but my guess is that if you don't, the arches will pull apart a little bit with time. Starting at the top

"These cages are traditionally planted with carnations, but I've found that many plants look great in them."

of the cage, remove the twist ties and lash each joint with a 6-inch piece of carpet thread, wrapping in both directions around the joint. The thread is easier to hold on to if you dampen it. Some of the lower intersections may be stiff enough that they don't need tying.

PLANTS FOR YOUR TRELLIS

In photos of English gardens, these cages are traditionally planted with carnations, but I've found that many plants look great in them. Select plants that bloom for a long time or plants that have attractive foliage over several seasons. I've planted the annual *Dianthus* 'Raspberry Parfait' in summer, and then replaced it with paperwhites for an indoor winter planting. Other tall annuals such as snapdragons (*Antirrhinum* spp.) work well. Sprawling plants such as moss verbena (*Verbena tenuisecta*) could clamber part of the way up the cage. Herbs such as Spanish lavender (*Lavandula stoechas* ssp. *pendunculata*), Salvia, and globe amaranth (*Gomphrena globosa*) would make an attractive, season-long display.

If you want to plant bulbs or young plants, carefully remove the cage and fill the pot to within 2 inches of the rim with a light soil mix. I use 1 part commercial potting soil to 1 part garden soil to 1 part compost or leaf mold. Set in your plants, and top with 1 inch of a light mulch, such as fine pine bark, to retain moisture. Carefully replace the cage.

Place the pots on a patio or deck, or even in a mixed border. I like to stick them right in a bed, set on a platform of eight weathered bricks. Four of these pots positioned around a sundial would give your garden a formal appearance. Wherever you put them, I think you'll find that their solid, organized look will bring order to any garden.

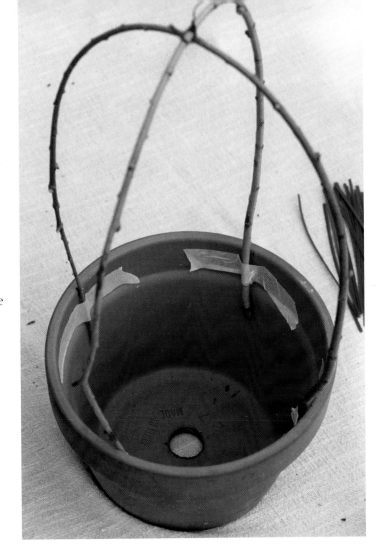

Twist ties hold the switches in place while you work.

Thin willow switches keep the ends of the hoops from moving around. Weave them in and out of the hoops right above the rim of the pot.

MARIO RODRIGUEZ

is a woodworker, writer, and teacher living in Haddonfield, New Jersey. He teaches woodworking courses at the Fashion Institute of Technology in New York City.

Build
a Classic
Planter Box

A simple planter box can spruce up a deck or terrace. This one for a shady site is filled with asparagus ferns, caladiums, licorice plant, yucca, and plectranthus.

NO MORE THAN 200 FEET from the Brooklyn-Queens Expressway and its constant traffic, our first home was a bona fide urban experience. We loved the energy of the city, but my wife—who was raised in rural New Jersey—yearned for a little bit of green as a counterpoint to the relentless browns, blacks, and grays of the city. Planter boxes for our rooftop terrace were the answer.

SIMPLE CONSTRUCTION WITH A FEW DETAILS

My custom furniture and woodworking business was just getting off the ground, so I didn't have a lot of time to spend on these boxes. Still, I wanted them to be both durable and stylish. My solution was to keep the construction simple—they're straightforward enough for even a novice woodworker—but to add a few details that give

Tools & Materials for Two Boxes

The tools required to make these planter boxes are fairly minimal, and you probably own many of them already. All materials listed can be found at a home center or in a good hardware store.

TOOL LIST

Portable drill

Handsaw

Jigsaw, with $\frac{1}{4}$-in. fine-tooth blade

Small bar clamp

Tape measure

Square

Counterbore bit, $\frac{1}{2}$ in. diameter

Miter box

Hammer

MATERIALS LIST

Two 8-ft.-long cedar or redwood 1x8s for the sides and ends.
(Wood is often sized nominally. These 1x8s, for example,
are actually only 7$\frac{1}{4}$ in. wide.)

One 8-ft.-long cedar $\frac{3}{4}$x8 for the bottoms

Tapered plugs ($\frac{1}{2}$ in. diameter, to fill counterbored holes)

Yellow carpenter's glue

One 4-ft.-long strip of square trim, $\frac{3}{4}$x1, for the ledger strips

Two 8-ft.-long pieces of $\frac{1}{2}$-in.-diameter half-round molding
(usually pine or some other softwood)

Galvanized 2$\frac{1}{2}$-in. deck screws

Galvanized 1-in. deck screws

Galvanized 3d finish nails

Sandpaper

Paint or stain (optional)

"My original boxes, still in good condition, are now well over 10 years old."

the box a lighter look and some grace. These details—cut-out bracket feet and a half-round molding—can be modified to suit your tastes.

Lumber is generally sold in 8-foot lengths, so you'll have less waste if you build two boxes instead of one. The total cost of materials is under $100, and they take only an afternoon or so to build.

BUILDING THE BOXES

Start by cutting the sides, ends, and ledger strips to length. Then use a pattern to trace the feet on the ends, and cut them out with a jigsaw. Use sandpaper to smooth any irregularities.

With 1-inch screws, attach an 8$\frac{1}{4}$-inch-long ledger strip to each end piece, just above the cutout for the bracket feet, to support the box bottom. Use a clamp to hold one side and one end together (with the side overlapping the end), then counterbore the holes for the 2$\frac{1}{2}$-inch screws and plugs. Screw the two pieces together, then do the same to the other side and end. Connect the L-shaped halves with screws.

Measure the length of the inside of the box, then cut the bottom to that length. Install the bottom, and attach it at each end by screwing two 1-inch screws to the ledger strips. Predrill the holes to avoid splitting the thin ledger strips. You'll be able to leave a gap of about $\frac{1}{2}$ inch on each side of the bottom to allow for drainage.

Smear a bit of glue inside the holes on the box sides, tap the plugs in place, and sand

1. Use a pattern to mark the feet, then cut them out with a jigsaw and touch up the rough edges with sandpaper.

2. A clamp holds everything in place when you screw the sides and ends together. Be sure to counterbore the holes for plugs.

3. The bottom slides inside the box and is secured in place with screws. There will be space on the sides to allow for drainage.

4. Plug the screw holes on the box side, then add the molding and some paint or stain (optional) for the finishing touches.

Standard Plastic Insert

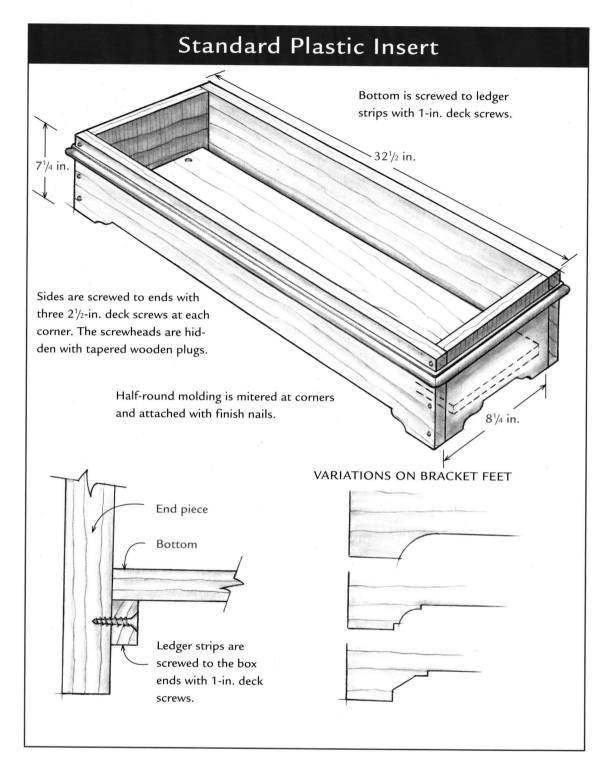

Bottom is screwed to ledger strips with 1-in. deck screws.

32½ in.

7¼ in.

Sides are screwed to ends with three 2½-in. deck screws at each corner. The screwheads are hidden with tapered wooden plugs.

Half-round molding is mitered at corners and attached with finish nails.

8¼ in.

End piece

Bottom

Ledger strips are screwed to the box ends with 1-in. deck screws.

VARIATIONS ON BRACKET FEET

them flush with the box. To trim, cut a miter on one end of a strip of molding. Hold it in position on the box and mark the far end. Then cut the molding to length and nail it in place. Repeat this process, working your way around the box. If you like, finish your box with paint or stain.

My original boxes, still in good condition, are now well over 10 years old, so they've been a good value. And they look just as nice overflowing with flowers on the patio of my suburban Tudor today as they did on the rooftop of that loft in Brooklyn.

HEATHER McCAIN

shares her passion for creating hanging baskets by teaching classes near Vancouver, British Columbia, Canada.

Create an Elegant Hanging Basket

Heather McCain tidies up a basket of "Supertunia" trailing petunias.

MY FAMILY TEASES ME ABOUT my passion for hanging baskets. In fact, I confess I've actually climbed lampposts all over British Columbia just to see how plants were arranged in hanging baskets.

I especially like baskets with one single type of plant blooming in just one hue. Saturated with color, they remind me of elegant jewels—an amethyst or ruby in a solo setting. They are also easy to design and construct. I recommend using a galvanized-wire frame lined with a wool mat or wood-fiber mat. These flexible materials retain moisture and keep roots cool yet allow them to breathe. In very dry areas, add a layer of landscape fabric or burlap for better moisture retention.

Long-trailing plants such as trailing petunias and trailing geraniums require only top planting. For short-trailing plants, plant on the sides of the basket as well as

Materials for a Hanging Basket

Wire-frame basket (16 inches across, 9 to 11 inches deep), plus hanger

Wood-fiber liner or wool mat liner to fit frame

1 meter of landscape fabric or burlap (for arid climates only)

8-inch plastic water saucer

51 inches of ½-inch clear-vinyl tubing

20 quarts of soil mix (16 quarts of lightweight, hanging-basket soil and 4 quarts of loam- or humus-based potting soil)

1 tablespoon kelp meal and 1 tablespoon lime

4 quarts of water

2 tablespoons slow-release, 15-15-15 fertilizer beads

Plants in 2½-inch pots: 13 short-trailing plants or 7 long trailing plants such as Supertunia, Surfina, or Wave petunias and trailing geraniums

Large container for mixing soil

Scissors, felt-tip pen, and small plastic bags

Sturdy bracket with a horizontal bar measuring 12 inches or more (to hang from a wall or post)

1½-inch screw hook, plus a swivel hook or an S hook, and a length of chain (to hang overhead)

"Look for plants with several stems, since they will produce prolific growth."

the top for a full-looking floral display. Choose plants based on where the basket will hang. Trailing *Begonia*, *Fuchsia*, and *Lobelia* are good in shaded baskets. Trailing *Petunia*, *Lantana*, and *Verbena* grow well in sunny spots.

Purchasing healthy plants is essential. I look for plants with several stems, since they will produce prolific growth. Plants in 2½-inch containers are easiest to insert through a wire frame.

Most soil mixes for hanging baskets are peat-based, and can be difficult to moisten after they dry out, so I add some loam- or humus-based potting soil, some lime to counter-act acidity from frequent watering and kelp meal for trace elements.

Baskets lose water through evaporation, so closely monitor their moisture level; in hot weather, check baskets daily. Water thoroughly, but allow baskets to dry out slightly between waterings.

Besides slow-release fertilizer at planting, I feed trailing petunias—those of the Supertunia, Surfinia, or Wave Series—every third watering with a 20-20-20 fertilizer that contains iron. These extra nutrients are needed for voluminous floral displays. In mid-July I check to see if the slow-release beads have dissolved. If they have, I add one tablespoon more. To keep your baskets blooming, remember to dead head regularly.

Assembling a Hanging Basket

1. Pad the basket's rim with vinyl tubing to prevent trailing stems from breaking. To do this, cut tubing into lengths to fit between the spaces for the hangers. Slit the tubing lengthwise with scissors, then wrap it around the rim.

2. Place a wood-fiber liner in the basket with the dark side facing out. Fold any excess liner material over the rim. Then place the water saucer inside the basket. Don't use a saucer for shade baskets in damp climates, since it may keep the basket too wet.

3. Mark the liner for side-planting of short-trailing plants. To designate planting positions, use a felt-tip pen to mark six dots evenly spaced around the basket about 3 inches from the rim. Cut an inverted T-shape slit in the liner about 2 inches by 2 inches at each dot.

4. Prepare 20 quarts of hanging-basket soil mix and moisten it with 4 quarts of water. Add soil mix to the basket, patting it down gently until it reaches 3 inches below the rim (one inch below the rim for top-planted baskets).

Note: For top-planted baskets with trailing petunias or trailing geraniums, skip Steps 3 and 6, and use only seven plants.

5. Thoroughly soak the plants by submerging the pots in water until all air bubbles disappear. This makes them more pliable for planting and helps them get established more quickly.

6. Insert plants through slits in the liner. Remove plants from containers, holding them by the root ball to protect the stems. Wrap root balls in small plastic bags to make insertion easier from outside the basket. From inside, pull root balls through so they rest on top of the soil. Remove the bag and anchor the root ball with a handful of soil.

7. Next, add soil to within an inch of the rim. Place one plant in the center, then space the other six around it, two inches or so from the edge. Firm the soil around the base of each plant. Sprinkle two tablespoons of slow-release fertilizer beads over the soil.

8. Attach hangers to the rim and hang the basket outside any time after your region's frost-free date. In hot, dry weather, water it immediately and hang it in the shade for a few days. In cool, damp weather, wait until it warms up before watering your basket thoroughly. Firm the soil around the roots of plants on the top layer after the first watering.

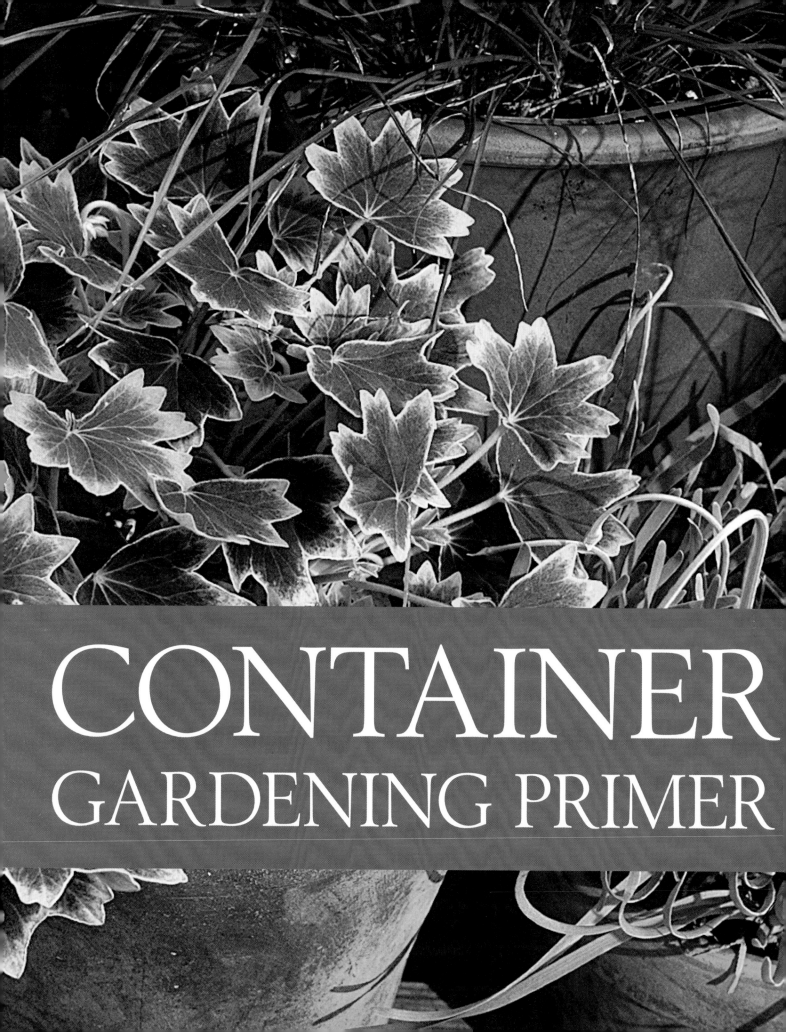

CONTAINER
GARDENING PRIMER

4

GROWING PLANTS IN CONTAINERS is a lot like growing them in the garden, but there are a few significant differences. For example, the soil you use. The best soil for most containers is actually a soilless mix. We'll take a look at its ingredients and how to vary these basic ingredients for the plants you're growing.

Also, container plantings need to be watered and fertilized more frequently. If you find that you have so many pots that you're becoming a slave to their watering regimen, a drip-irrigation system could be your best solution. And finally, if your plants outgrow their pots or become too large to haul in for the winter, we'll show you how to repot them and take cuttings so you can keep all your favorite plants going from year to year.

RITA BUCHANAN

is an avid gardener and the author of numerous books and articles on plants, gardening, and landscaping.

Evaluating *Potting* Soil

Ready-mixed potting soil offers convenience, but how do you decide which kind to use? Compare mixes with ideal standards.

WHETHER YOU'RE GROWING African violets on the windowsill, cherry tomatoes on the patio, or fuchsias in a hanging basket, to grow plants in pots you need potting soil. Chances are you can't just dig it from the garden—it's a rare achievement to have garden soil that's crumbly and porous enough to provide good drainage in a pot. More than likely you'll need to make or buy some.

Old-time gardeners made their own potting soil. The recipe was simple: one part loamy garden soil, one part compost or peat moss, and one part coarse sand. Homemade potting soil is good stuff, like home-baked bread, but busy modern gardeners often rely on store-bought products. Any local garden center has an assortment of bagged products labeled "potting soil." The question is, how do you know which to buy? Unlike food products, potting soils don't carry lists of ingredients on the label. You probably won't know what you've bought until you open the bag at home.

Most professional-grade, nationally marketed potting soils don't contain any *real* soil at all. They're "soilless" mixes, generally composed of peat moss, ground pine bark, and vermiculite and/or perlite, with lime and nutrients added.

The proliferation of mixes can be confusing. Some gardeners prefer to use special mixes for different kinds of plants. I make custom mixes when I'm feeling solicitous toward favorite plants, but I really don't think it's necessary. Commercial growers know you can pot a majority of plants in the same kind of soil and grow them successfully. This ideal mix is defined not by its list of ingredients—several formulas approach the ideal—but by its physical and chemical characteristics.

Whether you buy bagged potting soil or prepare your own, there are advantages to using the same mix for as many of your plants as possible (I make exceptions for orchids, bromeliads, cacti, and tiny seedlings). Standardizing the soil simplifies your watering, fertilizing, and repotting routines. And buying larger quantities of one mix is more economical than choosing several small bags of different mixes.

Whenever I try a new mix, commercial or homemade, I judge it against the set of standards that defines my ideal. This is a shortcut compared to potting up a few plants and watching their response. Assessing the physical characteristics of a soil mix is fairly straightforward—I do a series of simple tests that use common equipment and common sense. It's harder to evaluate a soil mix's chemical characteristics at home—that's what soil-test labs do—but there are some steps you can take.

To measure the porosity of potting soil, add water, then drain it off. With an ideal sample, you can add about two cups of water to a quart of dry soil. A few minutes later you can drain off about one cup of water. The volume of water that drains off equals the amount of air space in the soil.

TEST POROSITY

One of the first things I check is porosity. In a recently watered pot of ideal potting soil, only one-half the volume will be filled with particles of mineral and organic matter. One-quarter of the volume will be filled with water, clinging in the small pores between particles, and one-quarter of the volume will be filled with air, which enters the larger pores as water drains out.

I determine porosity by filling a jar with dry soil, measuring how much water can be added before it overflows, and then tipping the container and measuring the volume of water that drains off within a few minutes. The volume of water that drains off equals the volume of air in the soil. The difference between the amount added and the amount drained off is the net volume of water in the soil. Ideally, you can add about two cups of water to a quart (four cups) of soil, then drain off one cup. In practice, some mixes accommodate more than two cups of water,

because some is absorbed into the particles, as well as clinging to the spaces between particles. As long as the minimum one-cup's worth of air space is available, it does no harm if the mix retains extra water.

LOOK AT PARTICLE SIZE

The next thing I check is particle size. Ideal potting soil doesn't have any large clods, pebbles, sticks, or chunks of debris, and it doesn't have any dust-fine particles either. I usually screen a sample with a ¼-inch-mesh sifter. Chunks that don't fit through the mesh are too big. Then I put the sample in a sifter with ¹⁄₁₆-inch- mesh. Tiny bits that pass through the fine mesh are too small. I'm satisfied if most of the particles fit the ¼-inch to ¹⁄₁₆-inch size range. A few larger chunks don't do any harm if the potting soil will be used to fill 6-inch or larger pots. But I don't like to see more than a dusting of particles pass through the fine-mesh screen. Particles that are too small sift into the spaces between

To measure particle size, sift a sample of soil through ¼-inch- and ¹⁄₁₆-inch-mesh screens. Ideally, most of the particles will pass through the coarser mesh (on the left), but not through the finer mesh (on the right).

To measure compactibility, observe what happens when you add water to or press down on a sample of potting soil. Both of these samples started out the same volume. Ideally, a sample should resist compression (on the left). Be careful with fluffy mixes that collapse under pressure (on the right)—once compacted, they hold too much water and too little air.

larger particles, creating a densely packed nonporous mix. Fine, silty sand is a frequent culprit in this regard.

TEST DRAINAGE

It's easy to water a pot of ideal soil. The water doesn't bead up on the surface. It penetrates quickly and much is absorbed as it flows through the pot. The excess drains out promptly. If water moves very slowly, it means that the mix's pores and particle sizes are too small. Don't try to judge peat-based mixes as they come from the bag, though; they're very dry and hard to wet initially. Add hot water and wait a few hours for it to penetrate the peat. Subsequent routine watering isn't difficult unless you let pots filled with these mixes get too dry. Some commercial mixes include chemical wetting agents that make it easier to wet the peat moss, but these chemicals are reported to damage the root tips of sensitive plants.

Most of the ingredients that are used in soilless mixes can absorb their own weight in water—they weigh twice as much, or more,

when wet as when dry. Mixes containing soil or sand may take up as much water, but they're much heavier to start with, so the difference isn't as marked. I like to weigh a potful when it's dry and again when it's wet, but you can simply lift a pot to feel the difference. If you stick with the same mix for all your plants, you'll soon be able to judge a pot's water needs just by hefting it.

An ideal potting soil remains evenly mixed and homogeneous over time, but there's a tendency for repeated waterings to stratify the contents of a pot. Some ingredients—Styrofoam, perlite, and sometimes flakes of bark—are so light that they float to the surface. The small, heavy particles settle into a denser layer at the bottom of the pot that tends to waterlog, while the large, light particles form an arid zone at the top. I water a sample pot of mix and check to see what rises and what, if anything, flows out the bottom. The less a mix stratifies, the better.

EVALUATE SOIL STABILITY

Ideal potting soil doesn't shrink or swell; it fills the same volume wet or dry. I wet a sample and check to see if it cracks or pulls away from the pot as it dries. It's hard to water soil that shrinks into a dry block, leaving a gap around the edge of the pot—water just flows through the crack without soaking into the soil. (To restore a shrunken soil mass to full volume, soak the entire pot in a bucket of water for an hour or so.)

Any soil mix will fluff up a little when you mix it and will settle down when you use it to pot a plant, but this change in volume should be minimal. It's hard to position a plant at the right depth in a fluffy mix that loses up to a third of its volume when compressed. Also, compressing a mix closes the pores that should ideally be open to air.

"Potting soil is cheap compared to the plants you buy and the time you spend growing them—it's false economy to let valuable plants languish in inferior soil."

I gently squeeze a damp sample to test it for compactibility. If it can be compressed by squeezing, it will eventually be compressed by watering and gravity.

CHECK FOR CONTAMINANTS

Potting soil should be free from insects and other arthropods, weed seeds, and disease-causing organisms. The peat moss, bark, perlite, and vermiculite used in soilless mixes are more or less sterile when they're bagged, but any mix is subject to contamination once the bag has been opened.

Sand and topsoil are the ingredients most likely to carry contaminants to a soil mix. Heating damp soil to a temperature of 180°F for 30 minutes will kill most pathogens. You can buy small electric steam pasteurizers from greenhouse-supply dealers, or heat soil in your oven or microwave. To be honest, I never pasteurize the sand, topsoil, or mixed potting soil that I use at home, and so far I've had only a few minor problems—occasionally seedlings damp off, annual weeds sprout up, or earthworms hatch inside a pot.

TEST SOIL PH

The recommended pH range for potting soils that contain real soil is about 6.0 to 6.5, and for soilless mixes about 5.5 to 6.0. I wet a sample with distilled water and use litmus paper to get an approximate pH reading.

The pH of a soil mix in a pot is likely to change over a period of months in response to the application of soluble fertilizers and to watering with acidic or alkaline water. (Water isn't necessarily neutral. My well water here

in Connecticut is an acid 4.5; in Texas where I used to live, the tap water was an alkaline 10.0.) Many plants can tolerate any soil pH between 5.0 and 8.5 if supplied with fertilizer that includes all the major, minor, and trace elements, but beyond that range plants often show signs of nutrient deficiency. Adding small amounts of dolomitic limestone or soil sulfur—about one teaspoon per gallon of soil—will raise or lower the pH, respectively. Sprinkle the material on the surface of the soil in a pot and water in well. It may take a week or more before the effect is noticeable.

The ideal potting soil maintains its original pH over time; it has a high buffer capacity, or ability to withstand changes. Unfortunately, this is where soilless mixes come up short, particularly for the hobbyist. Large-scale greenhouses can afford the testing equipment that measures soil chemistry, but most homeowners can't and don't want to bother. I think the easiest way to improve a potting soil's buffer capacity is to add 5 percent to 10 percent by volume of loamy garden soil. After using soilless mixes exclusively for several years, I've started including real soil, and it makes a welcome difference in how long the pH stays at an acceptable level. I gather crumbly, compost-enriched soil from my vegetable garden, spread it on newspaper to dry, and then sift it through a 1/4-inch-mesh screen. If I didn't have a garden, I'd use the best topsoil I could buy.

What's in Soilless Mixes

Bark   Sphagnum moss   Reed sedge peat

Vermiculite   Perlite   Sand

Most of the commercial ready-mixed potting soils available today have been developed from formulas originated at Cornell University and the University of California, and combine two or more of the ingredients described below. The label on a bag of potting soil rarely specifies the identity and proportion of its ingredients, but once you open the bag, you can easily recognize the major components. The ingredients in soilless mixes may function to retain nutrients, but none are a major source of plant nutrients. Some soilless mixes are amended with an initial supply of fertilizers and trace elements; most include some form of lime to balance the pH.

SPHAGNUM MOSS

An abundance of terms—sphagnum moss, sphagnum peat, peat moss, peat, Canadian peat moss, and reed-sedge peat—refer to a group of products mined from boggy areas. Sphagnum moss is a rather coarse-textured moss that forms wide, flat colonies in freshwater bogs. The plants are slow-growing perennials that form a half-inch or so layer of fresh green growth each year. The old growth, lower on the stems, gradually darkens from yellowish-tan to brown, and eventually to a dark brownish black, as it's compressed and decomposed over time. Old, dark, dead sphagnum moss is called peat moss, sphagnum peat, or simply peat. Canadian peat moss is simply peat moss collected in Canada, as opposed to Scandinavian or continental U.S. peat moss. Reed-sedge peat is different stuff—

it's dead reeds, sedges, cattails, and similar marsh plants. If relatively young, it's coarse-textured with lots of visible stems. It quickly decomposes in a fine-textured, dense, humusy muck. Although inexpensive, reed-sedge peat is less desirable than sphagnum moss peat.

All forms of sphagnum moss and peat are acidic; limestone is added to counteract this acidity in a potting mix. All forms of peat absorb and retain water well. Younger, less decomposed, lighter-colored, coarser-textured products provide better aeration than do older, darker, fine-textured peats, which have few large pores for air to penetrate.

BARK PRODUCTS

Using tree-bark products in soilless mixes solves two problems: it's a less expensive alternative to peat moss, and it makes use of an otherwise wasted by-product of the timber industry. Bark-based mixes are especially popular in southern, Rocky Mountain, and Pacific states. Pine bark (from several species of pines) is most widely used, but some use has been made of hardwood bark and redwood sawdust.

Before it's added to a potting-soil mix, any kind of bark product is ground into ½-inch or smaller chips. Most processors then compost the bark, supplementing it with nitrogen to stimulate microbial activity. Recent research suggests that composted pine bark has antifungal properties and that plants potted in bark-based mixes are less susceptible to root rot. Bark products do not absorb or retain water or nutrients as well as sphagnum moss or peat products do. Bark-based mixes tend to provide better aeration than peat-based mixes do, but dry out more quickly. Lime is added to counteract the bark's acidity.

OTHER COMPOSTS

Other kinds of composted plant products are finding their way into potting-soil mixes in some parts of the country. These include feedlot manure, peanut hulls, sugar-cane stems, and other agricultural by-products; and leaves, yard wastes, or sewage sludge composted by municipalities. Most of these products are newly available and haven't been widely tested, but they show promise.

PERLITE

Perlite is a glassy, white volcanic rock that's been crushed and heated to about 1,800°F. Heating makes the rock expand like popcorn; as a result, perlite is very lightweight. It comes in small, irregular, sharp-edged particles that don't compact or decay. Water clings to the surface of the particles, but isn't absorbed by them. The pH is roughly neutral, and nutrient value is insignificant.

VERMICULITE

Vermiculite is produced by heating mica, a mineral that's naturally layered like the pages of a book, to a temperature of 1,400°F. Heating causes the layers to separate, and the result is a lightweight puffy material. Handled gently, vermiculite provides plenty of air spaces in a mix, but, unfortunately, if you press down on wet vermiculite, you can easily squeeze it into an irreversibly dense, compact, waterlogged mess.

A measure of dry vermiculite weighs about the same as dry perlite, but the vermiculite can absorb more water and nutrients. Vermiculite supplies potassium and magnesium, essential plant nutrients, and has a near-neutral pH.

STYROFOAM

White beads, usually ⅛ inch to ¼ inch in diameter, of Styrofoam plastic are used in some commercial potting mixes as a substitute for perlite. Styrofoam serves as a space filler, and little more. I can't think of any advantages to using Styrofoam; a major disadvantage is its tendency to float to the surface of a pot rather than stay integrated in the soil mix.

SAND

There's sand, and then there's sand. Horticulturists debate the value of rounded versus angular particles, quarry sand versus dune sand, and so on. I don't think any of that matters so much as the particle size. The coarser, the better. Fine sand settles into the spaces between other ingredients and makes a dense mix that excludes air. When I make my own mixes, I only use sand that's too coarse to pass through a window-screen sieve (1/16-inch mesh). Clean, washed sand has a near-neutral pH and little if any nutrient value. Sand is much heavier than any other ingredient used in potting soils. The added weight is an advantage for tall, top-heavy plants that might otherwise blow or tip over, but it's a disadvantage when you have to carry or move the potted plants.

Some potting-soil mixes contain high levels of fertilizers and soluble salts; others don't. This information is rarely specified on the bag. An easy way to reduce uncertainty is to leach out excess elements by running plenty of water through the soil when you pot a plant.

WILL IT RETAIN NUTRIENTS?

Whether or not a potting soil contains an initial charge of plant growth nutrients doesn't matter much to me, since it's so easy to meet a plant's requirements with regular doses of water-soluble fertilizer. More important than what a potting soil starts with is its ability to retain nutrients and slowly release them to the plant. This ability depends on the ingredients in the mix and can't be simply measured, but like buffer capacity, it can easily be increased by adding a small amount of loamy garden soil. Ideal potting soil can retain a supply of nutrients for weeks or months, depending on the plant's needs.

Usually it's hard to tell from the bag whether or not a commercial potting soil contains nutrients, and in what proportions and amounts. Adding more uncertainty, some mixes contain high levels of soluble salt compounds that aren't needed as plant nutrients, and may even be damaging to roots. Soil labs have equipment for testing nutrient and soluble-salt levels, but accurate test equipment is too expensive for my budget. Unless I'm familiar with a mix and know how plants respond to the nutrients it contains, I normally prefer to leach it out and start from scratch. To leach most of the initial nutrients and salts from commercial potting soil, run extra doses of water through the pot at the time you pot a plant (this helps settle the soil in around the root, too). A few weeks later, start a regular fertilizing program.

SHOP SMART

Potting soil is cheap compared to the plants you buy and the time you spend growing them—it's false economy to let valuable plants languish in inferior soil. If you're disappointed with what you find in a bag, dump it into the garden. At worst, it's an expensive garden-soil amendment; at best, you'll avoid problems with your potted plants.

If there's a nursery in your area growing plants you admire, ask them what kind of soil they're using and if they'll sell you some. Whether they mix their own or use ready-mixed, they've probably scouted out the most consistent, economical supply. The nursery staff can answer your questions on the best way to water and fertilize plants in that soil mix. Plants you buy from that nursery will have an easy adjustment if you repot them with the same soil they're used to.

Whether or not you buy through a friendly nursery, I'd recommend purchasing soil that's designed for professional growers. (One way to judge is by the type of information on the label—does it read like it was written by a horticulturist, or on Madison Avenue?) The reason is simple. State and federal regulations don't govern potting-soil quality; market feedback does. Companies that supply commercial growers have in-house testing labs that regularly monitor their product. They have to, because their customers demand it. Nurseries depend on the success of their crops, and can't risk losses due to inferior or inconsistent soil.

> *"When you find a mix you like, buy it in quantity to get the best price."*

Companies that market primarily to home gardeners may maintain the same high standards, but they don't get the same kind of feedback. Ask yourself, have you ever complained about a bum bag of potting soil? Rest assured that any nursery that loses a $10,000 crop will make a fuss. Along these lines, I usually buy nationally distributed rather than local brands, because I think the bigger companies invest more in quality control.

It may be hard to find more than one brand of professional-grade soil at any particular garden center. If you want to try different brands, you may have to shop in several places. In remote areas, it may be convenient to mail-order from greenhouse-supply companies. Catalog prices for major brands look low until you add on the shipping charges; then the cost is about the same whether you buy mail-order or shop locally.

When you find a mix you like, buy it in quantity to get the best price—a 40-pound bale may cost only three or four times as much as a 4-pound bag. Share the savings by shopping with a gardening friend, or stockpile the surplus for future use. Kept dry, most mixes can be stored indefinitely. However, don't store bags of wet potting soil, particularly in warm weather—particles of peat and bark begin to decompose, and the soil's pH and fertility are liable to change for the worse. For the same reason, don't buy broken bags that have been stored outdoors in the rain and sun.

STEVE SILK

is a contributing editor for *Fine Gardening*. His passion for gardening includes photography, lecturing, and crafting outdoor furniture for the garden.

Drip
Irrigation
Makes Watering
a Cinch

Watering all of these pot-grown plants, once a time-consuming chore, now takes the author less than a minute, thanks to a well-concealed drip irrigation system.

THANKS TO LAST SUMMER'S drought, I lost a passel of plants. But the biggest casualty was my free time. It seems as if I spent every available minute out on the patio with hose in hand, trickling water into the 50 or so parched pots that housed my favorite finds. Even during a rainy summer, they require a lot of watering and fertilizing. But that thirsty summer pushed me over the edge; I finally broke down and installed a drip irrigation system for my containers.

I spent about $50 and several hours putting it all together, but the results—and the time it has saved me on a daily basis—are worth far more. Drip irrigation is something I now recommend to anyone who tends a lot of pots. But before you plunge in, here's a significant caveat: You'll want to use drip irrigation in a place where you'll be able to keep its attendant water lines hidden from sight and out of the way of foot traffic, errant weed

Especially thirsty plants like this canna are outfitted with multiple emitters so they get plenty of water. The author monitored his system for a couple of weeks to make sure water levels were right.

whackers, and lawnmowers. Since I display most of my plants against the south wall of the house, I hid the system between the wall and the containers. On a deck, you could run the water supply lines beneath the decking and up through the cracks between boards.

BUILD A SYSTEM TO FIT YOUR NEEDS

The trick was assembling a system that could meet the needs of all my plants, from water- and fertilizer-grubbing tropicals like *Brugmansia* and *Canna* to more self-reliant desert dwellers such as *Echeveria* and *Agave*. And, since my display changes during each season and from year to year, I needed an adaptable system so I could move things about.

My rush to escape the daily drudgery of watering led me to purchase a drip irrigation kit designed for container plants. In one package I got all the basics: a device that couples the system to a hose bib, a length of hose ½-inch or so in diameter to pipe water throughout the designated area, sections of ¼-inch feeder tubing to relay water from the hose to any number of pots, assorted connectors to link lengths of tubing, and scores of emitters—the gizmos that control how much water actually gets delivered to a given spot. If you have municipal water, and if all your plants have similar water requirements, one of these kits may be all you need. But a diverse collection of plants requires a wider range of emitters than the kit provides. And with well water, you'll need a special filter to prevent debris from clogging the system.

SETUP IS A SNAP

Assembling a drip irrigation system is as simple as snapping together a set of Tinkertoys. Even components made by different manufacturers can be incorporated into a single

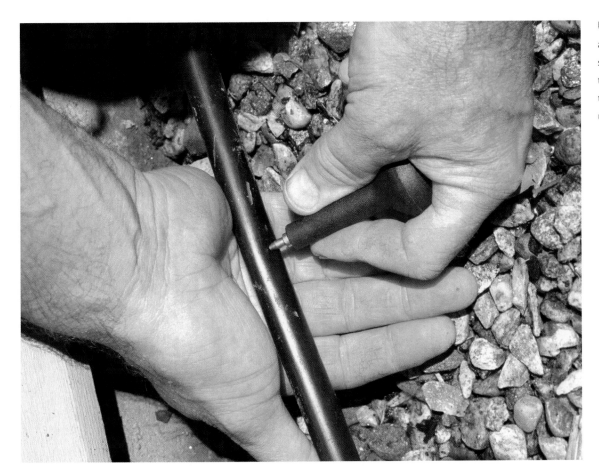

Use a hole-punch or a nail to perforate the system's main hose, then attach feeder tubing to water individual pots.

drip system. The first step is to put all the hose and tubing—typically made of black plastic—out in the sun so the heat will make them pliable and thus easier to position. Run a length of the hose from a water outlet to a point just beyond where you'll need water. Be generous—a little extra hose at the end helps when crimping the main line shut after everything's installed and again at season's end, when you reopen the hose and flush the system out. Don't worry about being too precise; you can make changes later.

Then use the hole-punch that comes with the kit or a 10-penny nail to perforate the hose near any spot you want to put a pot. Plug a connector (a barbed plastic tube that carries water from one section of hose or tubing to another) into each hole and attach enough feeder tubing to reach the container. Since I wanted my system to be adaptable, I

sized the feeder tubing generously, giving each line about 50 percent more length than needed. Again, there's no need to be overly precise—you can always extend a length of tube or cut it back. You could lay all the lines out at once then insert emitters as needed, but I found it easier to work from one end to the other, installing tubing and deploying emitters as I went.

GET THE WATER FLOW RIGHT

Plugging in an emitter is easy, but selecting one that will precisely meet a plant's needs is not. Emitters come in a variety of capacities, including models that deliver ½ gallon per hour (gph), 1 gph, 2 gph, and adjustable units that can deliver up to 10 gph. There's also soaker tubing, which emits a specific amount of water for each foot of length. The water needs of my containers vary wildly, but

A round emitter determines how much water will be delivered to the pot. Emitters are available in a range of capacities.

thanks to all that hand watering, I knew about how much each pot needed.

My goal was to establish a watering level that would serve the greatest number of containers, and then adjust the rest of the system to deliver more or less water as needed. Most of my plants happened to be of moderate thirst, so I outfitted them with emitters of middling capacity. Each one got a single 2-gph emitter that I mounted on a plastic stake and stuck into the pot so that the emitter stood an inch or two above soil level to reduce the chance of clogging. This left me with lots of room to play with the amount of water delivered to the other containers.

❧

"Assembling a drip irrigation system is as simple as snapping together a set of Tinkertoys."

Desert plants got either a 1-gph or a ½-gph emitter each, while thirstier plantings, thanks to extra tubing and multiple outlet connectors (called T-connectors), got multiple emitters as I deemed appropriate. The thirstiest plants got adjustable emitters capable of dousing their pots with up to 10 gph.

During the installation, I kept a tally of the number of gallons per hour the system would need to dispense. If that hourly total exceeds your household's hourly water-delivery capacity, the irrigation system won't work properly. You can roughly calculate how much water your household delivers by turning on the hose and measuring how much water gushes out in one minute. Multiply that amount by 60 to establish an hourly rate. Should the system's demand exceed your supply, install smaller-capacity emitters throughout and just leave the hose on for a longer period of time, or set up multiple systems and irrigate, say, half the plants at a time.

Once my basic system was in place, I turned on the water briefly to flush any debris from the system, then folded and clamped the far end of the main hose shut and turned the water back on to determine how much water would be enough. As the system filled with water, pressure evened, and the emitters delivered water at a fixed rate. I let the water flow until it came out the bottom of the moderately thirsty containers. Then I examined the others. Were they getting enough water or too much? I made modifications accordingly, adding an emitter here, using a smaller capacity one there, or

opening or closing the adjustable emitters a bit at a time. I continued to monitor my plantings closely over the next week or so, fine tuning and making sure none of the emitters fell out of the their pots. If emitters or feeder tubes are popping off, your water pressure is too high. Most drip-system manu-facturers sell devices to reduce water pressure.

Once the containers were getting optimal watering, I started to add an occasional dose of fertilizer. Most drip systems can be equipped with a device that holds, dilutes, and automatically delivers fertilizer along with the water. After that, I was home free. I'd walk out back, flip on the water, and a half-hour later I'd walk back and turn it off. My actual effort at watering and fertilizing about 50 containers took less than a minute a day. Now that's low-maintenance gardening.

Use T-connectors and extra tubing to either water multiple pots off one feeder tube or add extra emitters to a container.

JAMES KRAMER

works for TrueLeaf Technologies in Petaluma, California, where he designs greenhouse control, irrigation, and heating systems.

A Simple Guide to Repotting Plants

Roots protruding from a pot's drainage hole is a sign that the plant needs to be repotted.

MOST HEALTHY CONTAINER-grown plants eventually outgrow the confines of their pots. A good way to reinvigorate a root-bound plant is to give it a new home—also known as repotting. In my former job as a greenhouse manager, I spent a lot of time giving plants new homes.

REPOT PLANTS IN SPRING OR SUMMER

Recognizing when it's time to repot is the first step. Telltale signs include soil that dries out quickly or has become degraded; roots tightly packed within a pot or protruding from drainage holes; and water sitting on the soil surface too long after watering. Often a plant simply looks top-heavy or as if it might burst out of its pot. The best time to repot most plants is when they're actively growing, in the spring or summer. However, plants can usually handle repotting whenever the situation warrants it.

WATER ROOT-BOUND PLANTS

The second step is to get a plant out of its pot. If a plant is root-bound, it helps to water the root ball thoroughly in advance. For plants in small to medium pots, invert the pot and support the top of the root ball with one hand. Put your other hand on the bottom of the pot and use a downward throwing motion with an abrupt stop. Many plants will slip out after one or two throws. If not, knock the edge of the pot against a sturdy surface, such as a potting bench, still holding the pot with both hands. It may take a few good whacks to release the plant, but be careful not to break the pot.

A plant ready for repotting should slide out with the soil in one piece (see the left photo below). If much of the soil falls free of the roots, the plant may not need repotting. If it does need repotting, there will likely be a solid soil-and-root mass in the shape of the just-removed pot. Roots should be white or light-colored. Black, dark-colored, or foul-smelling roots are usually signs of a serious problem, such as fungal disease.

TRIM AND LOOSEN ROOTS

Roots packed tightly in a pot don't take up nutrients efficiently. To promote good nutrient absorption, trim the roots and loosen up the root ball before replanting. Use a sharp knife or pruning shears for this job, removing as much as the bottom third of the root ball if necessary (see the right photo below).

Root-bound plants should slip out of their pots relatively easily; watering first will help.

Trim roots to increase nutrient absorption.

Combing through a plant's roots will also help loosen up the root ball and promote better nutrient uptake.

A paper towel effectively keeps soil in the pot while letting excess water drain out.

Don't be surprised if what you cut off is a thick tangle of root tissue. Also make three or four vertical cuts up to a third of the way into the remaining root ball. Cut through any roots growing in a circular pattern to help prevent the plant from strangling itself with its own roots as it grows. If the roots are thick along the sides of the root ball, shave or peel away the outer layer. Or gently untangle the root ball with your fingers as if you were mussing someone's hair. Do this along the top edge of the root ball, too.

The new pot's size depends on the plant and its potential growth rate, how well it's growing under current conditions, and the ultimate size desired for the plant. Rely on your own idea of what a healthy specimen of a particular species should look like. When in doubt, go with a pot the next size up.

POSITION THE ROOT BALL JUST BELOW THE RIM

To keep soil from leaking out the bottom of the pot, cover its drainage holes with a paper towel, coffee filter, mesh screen, or pot shard. If you use a pot shard, place it convex side up to avoid sealing the hole. While it's common practice to put gravel or charcoal in the bottom of pots, they don't help with drainage and take up valuable space, so I don't recommend using them.

To repot a small plant that's easy to lift, put a few inches of moist soil in the pot and tamp it down lightly. Place the plant in the pot, centering it. The goal is to get the top of the root ball to sit an inch or two below the rim of the pot. If the plant is in too deep, gently raise it and add more soil. If it sits too

Position your plant an inch or two below the pot's rim.

high, remove the plant and dig out some soil, or just dump the soil out and start over.

LEAVE SOME ROOM FOR WATER

Now, fill the space around the root ball with soil. I've noticed that there are two approaches to this job—"stuffing" and "filling." Stuffers like to press soil in around a plant. Fillers like to fill the pot to the brim and let the soil settle in during the first few waterings. I'm usually a filler, but I do stuff a bit at times, especially with top-heavy plants that need to be steadied. Whether you stuff or fill, leave some room at the top so the pot can hold enough water with each watering to thoroughly moisten the soil.

Finally, trim the plant's foliage relative to how much the roots were pruned. In other words, if you removed a third of the roots, prune off a third of the top growth as well. Water the plant thoroughly and keep it moist, shaded, cool, and perhaps misted until it is reestablished.

Whether you "stuff" or "fill" your pot with soil, leave enough room so the pot can hold water.

SYDNEY EDDISON

is a long-time contributor to *Fine Gardening*. She has written numerous gardening books including, *The Self-Taught Gardener*.

Tending
Tender
Plants *in Winter*

Rid plants of aphids and other pests by spraying them with a strong jet of water. A sink sprayer works well for smaller plants.

DURING THE LAST DECADE , I've become fascinated with growing annuals and tender perennials in containers on my patio. By September, Mexican flame vine (*Senecio confusus*) sprawls over the paving, *Plectranthus* and coleus (*Solenostemon scutellariodes*) are bushlike in stature, and angels' trumpets (*Brugmansia* spp.) are the size of trees.

It would be daunting to bring these lush plants inside. We don't have a greenhouse, and many of the plants are simply too heavy to move. Instead, I take cuttings, root them in water, and overwinter them in a spare room.

EASY-DOES-IT PROPAGATION

My quick-and-easy propagating method was born of desperation the first year I grew a 'Charles Grimaldi' angels' trumpet. I loved this plant above all others. Its silken trumpets are apricot-colored and exquisitely creased and

The author turned a spare bedroom into a winter haven for tender plants. She augments sunlight with fluorescent lights.

folded into pale green calyces. By day, they hang beneath the leafy canopy, but at dusk, they flare upward and outward, releasing a sweet, sultry perfume.

Because I couldn't bear to lose this treasure, I asked my plant-collecting friend Gary Keim how to take cuttings. He told me to use sharp pruners to cut 6- to 8-inch shoots without flower buds. With frost breathing down my neck, I hastily stuck the shoots in a glass of water. Within a few days, white spots began to appear on the stems, and roots soon emerged at these points.

Emboldened by success, I began rooting other soft-stemmed plants in water, including *Plectranthus*, coleus, and geraniums (*Pelargonium* spp.). I cut stems just below a

pair of leaves, remove the lower leaves, and put the cuttings in glasses or bottles. The roots usually appear at the leaf nodes. After filling the containers with water to below the remaining leaves, I set them away from direct sunlight. North-facing windowsills work well. Coleus roots in about a week and most others within two weeks. After several roots emerge, I transfer them to 4- or 6-inch pots partially filled with commercial potting soil. I add potting soil to within half an inch of the top, tapping the pots after each addition, and water thoroughly.

A WINTER HOME FOR PLANTS

To accommodate the cuttings, we turned our extra guest room into the plant room. It has two south-facing and two west-facing windows. In our drafty, old 19th-century farmhouse, there's good air circulation, and with the radiators in this room turned off, the temperatures approximate those of a cool greenhouse (50°F at night and about 65°F by day). A glassed-in porch where the temperature doesn't drop below 40°F would also work well.

We did make some adjustments. Our windows don't admit enough light for sun-loving plants like angel's trumpets, and the window sills are too narrow for 6-inch pots. My husband made a simple trestle table the same height as the window sills from three 8-foot-long, 2x10-inch planks placed on two sawhorses. To improve the light, he installed two sets of shop-light fixtures with full-spectrum fluorescent tubes, suspended on chains so they can be raised and lowered. Plant leaves should be at least 10 inches from the lights. I sometimes create makeshift platforms to get plants the right distance from the lights, and I use a timer to keep the lights on 12 hours a day.

Here are two tips for overwintering plants indoors: Avoid crowding—plants need good air circulation—and choose the right plants for the exposure. East, west, and south exposures are best for flowering plants, while foliage plants do best in a north-facing window.

Overall, temperature is less critical than light. But coleus, which needs less light and warmer temperatures, suffers through winter in our plant room. Many other plants prefer it cool, and when the outdoor temperature goes above 40°F, I open the window at the opposite end of the room. The plants also enjoy the fresh air.

WATER PLANTS ONLY WHEN DRY

Plants growing slowly in winter need less water. To tell when a plant needs water, stick a finger in the pot. If the soil is dry, water the plant thoroughly—you should see water dripping through the drain holes, but never let the pot sit in standing water. A rule of thumb is that the smaller the pot, the more often you'll have to water.

Indoor plants also need regular feeding. You can either use water-soluble fertilizer once a month according to its directions, or a very diluted solution of fertilizer every time you water. I prefer the constant weak dose; it's easier on my memory. I put ¼ teaspoon of a 20-20-20 fertilizer in a 2-quart watering can and keep it near the plants.

TREAT PLANTS AT THE FIRST SIGN OF PESTS

Other than watering and feeding, plants need little care in winter. I do watch for aphids and, horror of horrors, spider mites, which often attack angel's trumpet. While mites are

> *"Other than watering and feeding, plants need little care in winter."*

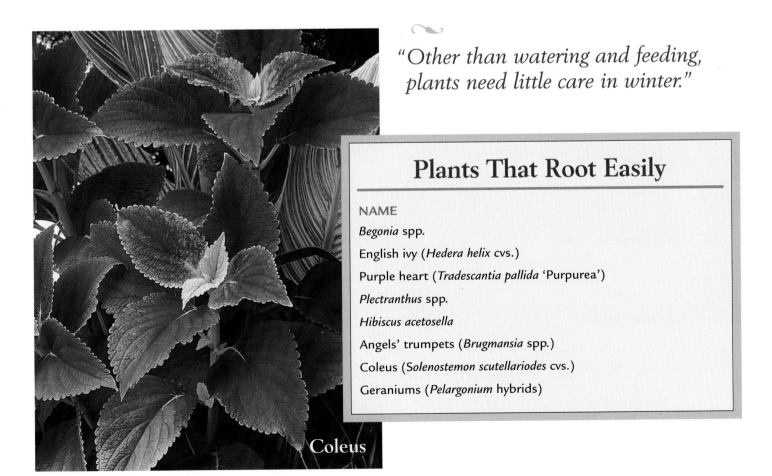

Coleus

Plants That Root Easily

NAME

Begonia spp.

English ivy (*Hedera helix* cvs.)

Purple heart (*Tradescantia pallida* 'Purpurea')

Plectranthus spp.

Hibiscus acetosella

Angels' trumpets (*Brugmansia* spp.)

Coleus (*Solenostemon scutellariodes* cvs.)

Geraniums (*Pelargonium* hybrids)

(ABOVE) Many soft-stemmed plants root easily in water.

(RIGHT) Rooted cuttings can then be potted up and
tended throughout the winter.

"The smaller the pot, the more often you'll have to water."

almost invisible to the naked eye, I become suspicious when a plant's leaves look yellowish. Spider mites suck the juices out of the leaves from the underside; if webs are visible between leaves and branches, an infestation has taken hold.

At the first sign of pests, I fill the kitchen sink with water and a teaspoon of liquid dish detergent. I secure the pot in a plastic bag to keep the soil in, invert it, and jounce the leaves up and down in the soap suds. Simply washing the leaves with a strong jet of water,

as from a hose or sink sprayer, also helps keep them bug-free.

By early spring, my cuttings are strapping plants, and the sooner I can get them outside, the better. In April, and sometimes as early as March, I start putting the most cold-tolerant plants, like angel's trumpet and *Fuchsia*, outside on the north side of the house. They get some early-morning sun, but it isn't hot enough to damage their tender leaves. At night, I bring them all in.

The indoor-outdoor regimen can be tedious, but it's worth it. You have to introduce these housebound plants to the outdoors gradually. Even sun-lovers must be exposed only to early-morning sun at first. That's why the north side of the house is a perfect spot, because they get morning sun in increasing doses as the season progresses. Once outside, well-acclimated plants are much less susceptible to pests.

If all this sounds like a lot of trouble, it really isn't. During the cold months, I usually visit the plant room daily just to make myself feel better. There's not much to do, except pick off a dead leaf or two and poke my fingers in the soil to see if the plants need a drink. In the spring, my container garden gets a big head start; I've saved a bit of money, and I've had the pleasure of enjoying my favorite tender plants all year.

Zonal geranium

GREAT CONTAINER
PLANTS

5

JUST ABOUT ANY PLANT WILL GROW in a container if you provide it with the right size pot, an appropriate potting mix, and the right site. But there are certain plants that just seem "made" for containers. We'll cover a few of those here so your container gardens will shine all year.

Why not fill your winter with grape hyacinths, crocus, or daffodils by tricking them into thinking it's spring? Or add summer-flowering bulbs to your containers rather than limiting yourself to just the springtime varieties? Roses, succulents, and even trees are all good candidates for containers. A Japanese maple, for instance, is quite a conversation piece when grown in a container. And if you've ever wanted to try creating an herb standard, we'll show you how to do it, step-by-step.

ROB PROCTOR

is a self-described gardening jack-of-all-trades, including writer, illustrator, and photographer. He is the Director of Horticulture at the Denver Botanic Gardens.

Summer-
Flowering
Bulbs

The white, seductively fragrant flowers of acidanthera, a summer-flowering bulb, rise above white wax begonias (*Begonia schulziana*), dead nettle (*Lamium* 'Silver Nancy'), and purple-leaved perilla (*Perilla frutescens* 'Atropurpurea').

MANY GARDENERS ASSUME that when the last tulip fades, the bulb season is over. They couldn't be further from the truth. Summer is the time to revel in a glorious wealth of fascinating lesser-known bulbs, such as acidanthera, crinum, and Aztec lily.

I look forward to the flowering of my favorite summer bulbs with great anticipation. Most are breathtakingly beautiful. Many, such as Peruvian daffodil (*Hymenocallis narcissiflora*), offer splendid scents, while others, such as pineapple lily (*Eucomis bicolor*), display striking foliage and architectural form.

Bulbs have been a passion of mine since I was a boy, and for the past decade I've been experimenting with every one I could find. (For simplicity's sake, I'll refer to all bulbous plants as bulbs, whether they are true bulbs, tubers, corms, or rhizomes.) Tender, summer-blooming

The tropical-looking flowers and foliage of pineapple lily are underplanted with globe amaranth (*Glomphrena globosa*). A South African native, pineapple lily blooms in midsummer.

bulbs are easy to plant and to coax into bloom. I'd like to tell you about some of my favorites.

Many summer-blooming bulbs originated in tropical or subtropical climates, and most are not hardy in regions colder than USDA Hardiness Zone 6. If left in the ground over the winter in cold regions, they will freeze and die. But that's no reason to avoid growing them. In cold climates like mine here in Denver, Colorado (Zone 5), tender, summer-flowering bulbs can be grown in containers

or in the ground if they're simply moved inside for winter storage in a protected place. In warmer climates, the bulbs can be left outdoors year-round, either in the ground or in pots.

PLACE POTS OF BULBS IN THE LANDSCAPE

Containers protect my tender bulbs during the winter and also extend the options of what I can grow. When I can't provide the conditions in the ground that certain bulbs

> *"Summer is the time to revel in a glorious wealth of fascinating lesser-known bulbs, such as acidanthera, crinum, and Aztec lily."*

⟿

require—excellent drainage, wet feet, or acidic soil, for example—I plant them in pots. There I can control the growing conditions, and I can place the containers where the plants will thrive best. I position the tuberoses (*Polianthes tuberosa*) where they can bake, the elephant ears (*Alocasia* spp.) where they can steam, and the Peruvian daffodils where they won't fry. Growing bulbs in pots also makes it easier to control slugs and rodents, the bane of bulb growers.

I grow dozens of pots of bulbs on my patios, along walkways, beneath windows, and near house doors and garden entrances. Bulbs combine beautifully with annuals, succulents, herbs, and tropical shrubs—sometimes in the same container.

I prefer mainly terra-cotta clay pots. They absorb and hold heat, mimicking the native climate of many summer bulbs. I soak clay pots after planting to prevent the dry clay from stealing moisture from the bulbs. I also use wooden containers, including bushel baskets, wine crates, and whiskey half-barrels that have holes drilled in them for drainage.

PLANT THE "NOSE" UP

The needs of summer-blooming bulbs—in the ground or in containers—are usually quite easy to satisfy.

Purchase your bulbs early for best selection, but wait until night temperatures have settled at about 50°F or above before you plant. I usually order in the depths of winter and request a midspring delivery; the beginning of April is ideal for me. I also buy bulbs from local garden centers then. In the South

and other warm-winter regions, you can plant earlier.

Most bulbs prefer a loose, well-drained soil. My garden has sandy loam, which I have supplemented with liberal amounts of compost. My soil is ideal for most bulbs, but it precludes growing moisture-loving bulbs in the borders. They go in pots.

I use ordinary, brand-name potting soil in containers, adding both play sand and small gravel. (I use approximately 1 part sand and gravel to 3 parts soil, but when I'm busy planting, I don't measure—I just use what feels right.) Crinums (*Crinum* × *powellii*) and a few other bulbs like wet feet, so they get compost or peat in their mix.

The pointed "nose," or growing tip, of the bulb should be planted facing up. If you can't find a tip, look for evidence of last year's roots—that end goes down. Most summer-blooming bulbs should be planted with 4 to 6 inches of soil over their noses, in the ground or in pots. If the soil is heavy, plant more shallowly.

I water my potted bulbs only when they need it. If the soil feels dry, I water. Container-grown bulbs need the most attention in July and early August, when their roots are starting to get crowded.

I fertilize about five times during the growing season, alternating between a balanced fertilizer, such as Miracle-Gro, and a fertilizer that's high in phosphorous (look for a formula like 8-59-9), to promote roots and more blooms. I don't fertilize my bulbs after the middle of August because the plants need to wind down and prepare for dormancy.

Favorite Summer Bulbs

ACIDANTHERA

Gladiolus callicanthus is native to Ethiopia and is often called acidanthera or Abyssinian gladiolus. It is hardy in the South and along the West Coast. Its spearlike leaves grow to 2½ feet tall. In late summer or autumn, they are topped by graceful, pure white blossoms that open wide to show deep maroon markings on the interior of the petals. The fragrance is heavenly, and the flowers are long-lasting when cut. The bulbs like sun, moisture, and well-drained soil, and they're suitable for beds or large pots. They must be well fed to produce flowers.

AMARCRINUM AND CRINUM

Both × *Amarcrinum* and *Crinum* produce showy, fragrant, pink or white, trumpet-shaped flowers up to 4 inches long, which rise on strong, leafless stems above glossy, straplike leaves. One of the most popular and easy-to-grow crinum lilies is *Crinum × powellii*, which has pink or white flowers. Amarcrinum blooms in late summer or early autumn. The cultivar 'Summer Maid' grows to about 2 feet tall, and its flowers, up to 10 per stem, are pink and stay in bloom for nearly a month.

Crinums and amarcrinums thrive in sun or partial shade. I grow them in large pots where the bulbs can multiply, because they bloom best when crowded. They resent transplanting and may not bloom the first year after planting. Plant them with the necks of the gourd-shaped bulbs exposed. Both are hardy in Southern states.

AZTEC LILY

Sprekelia formosissima is sometimes called Aztec lily, perhaps for its blood-red color and its Mexican origin. Each stem, less than 1 foot tall, bears a solitary blossom above clumps of thin foliage. It usually blooms in early summer; established clumps may bloom again later in the summer. Provide partial sun and abundant moisture. Because the bulbs are tender and bloom best when crowded, container culture is probably best.

MONTBRETIA

The old-fashioned montbretia (*Crocosmia × crocosmiiflora*) looks like a small gladiolus until it begins to bloom in late summer. Then its orange, gold, or yellow star-shaped flowers are held in a graceful manner on thin, arching, zigzag stems. Montbretias can be treated just like acidantheras. The corms are considered tender—they thrive in West Coast gardens—but have proved surprisingly tough here in Denver, sometimes lasting for several years in the garden without extra protection.

PERUVIAN DAFFODIL

The sweetly scented Peruvian daffodil (*Hymenocallis narcissiflora*) blooms in early summer with white or pale yellow flowers of great beauty. The recurving petals accent a daffodil-like cup. The flowers appear on leafless stems, 1 foot or more tall, over long, arching foliage. Part sun and moist, well-drained soil are best. The bulbs may be grown in the ground or in pots, and should be planted with just the tip exposed.

PINEAPPLE LILY

The well-named pineapple lily (*Eucomis bicolor*) offers a conical arrangement of flowers topped by a tuft of green leaves. The individual flowers—many hundreds to a stem—are pale green with pink or purple stripes. They bloom in midsummer on thick stems, about 18 inches high, above long, broad leaves of glossy, light green. The flowers of the pineapple lily last for a month or more and are followed by green seedpods that barely alter the "pineapple" arrangement, so the plant is showy for three months or more. The species *E. autumnalis* blooms a little later and has wavy leaf margins. I plant them three to a large clay pot or bushel basket.

Most summer-flowering bulbs are relatively pest- and disease-free if they are grown under suitable conditions. If a plant is frequently plagued with problems, it may need a new location, more or less water, or a trip to the compost pile.

OVERWINTERING BULBS

Where your bulbs spend the winter depends on your climate. If you garden in a mild climate, your bulbs can winter over in the garden or in pots outdoors. Some will remain evergreen; others will die back.

If you garden in an area with cold winters, you need to protect tender bulbs by bringing them indoors. After frost blackens the foliage, cut it back and dig the bulbs from garden beds or from pots that are too large to move indoors. Shake off most of the soil clinging to the roots. Spread the bulbs on newspaper to dry for a few days, then bag them in labeled mesh or paper sacks. I sometimes pack bulbs in wood shavings to keep them from touching.

I overwinter many bulbs right in their pots. It's easy to whisk the pots indoors when temperatures plummet in autumn and deal with them later (although "whisk" may not be the right word to describe hauling in 50 or 60 clay pots). Some potted bulbs, including amarcrinum (× *Amarcrinum*) and crinum, will stay green all winter indoors in a well-lighted place, such as a sun porch.

I store the bags and pots of bulbs in my basement, which stays about 50°F, approximately the winter temperature that many of these bulbs would experience in their homelands. Root cellars, attics, or unheated garages may also provide suitable storage.

I keep an eye on the bulbs during storage, checking for rot, fungus, or desiccation. If loose bulbs wither too much, I sprinkle them

with a bit of water. If the soil in a container feels bone-dry, I water lightly.

Overwintered bulbs will start to show signs of life again by spring. Loose bulbs can be potted up when they begin to sprout, or they can be kept in storage until it's time to plant outdoors in the garden. When new shoots poke up in overwintered containers, replace the top 2 inches of soil with fresh soil, and begin your usual watering and feeding regimen. In cold-winter regions, put the pots under lights or move them to a sun porch until the weather warms up. I move them outside about the time I plant out annuals, in late April. Handled properly, most summer-flowering bulbs will increase, multiply, or produce bigger plants from year to year.

The pink flowers of amarcrinum, which bloom in late summer, tower over the purple leaves of flowering kale and other bulbs in a garden of container-grown plants.

Scissors are the author's pruning
shears of choice for standards
with tiny leaves like myrtle or
rosemary.

DENISE SMITH

owns GardenSmith Nursery & Greenhouse in Jefferson, Georgia, where she grows and sells herbal standards, herbs, vegetables, annuals perennials, tropicals, and unusual plants.

Grow
Your Own Herb
Standard

This rosemary standard has a strong, straight stem critical to creating a standard.

N O MATTER WHAT THE SIZE or style of a garden, there is always a spot for an herb standard. Whether it's a matching pair flanking a formal entrance, an eclectic grouping in a border, or a single specimen in the center of your picnic table, standards are a great way to add interest to your garden.

A standard—usually a plant with a single, straight stem and a tuft of foliage on top—is a form of topiary, or the trimming of plants into ornamental shapes. Ball-, cone-, and animal-shaped plants are also considered topiaries. Most often grown in pots, topiaries can be moved for routine maintenance or to create focal points in the garden.

LOOK FOR SINGLE, STRAIGHT STEMS

Plants with single, straight stems, opposite branching, and short internodes—the space between branches—are

Plants for Standards

Anisodontea

Basil (*ocimum basilicum*)

Flowering maple (*Abutilon*)

Lavender (*Lavandula dentata*)

Licorice plant (*Helichrysum petiolare*)

Myrtle (*Myrtus communis*)

Rosemary (*Rosmarinus officinalis*)

Scented geraniums (*Pelargonium* spp.)

Sterile coleus (*Solenostamon scuttellariodes*)

the easiest to work with. Rosemary (*Rosmarinus officinalis*), myrtle (*Myrtus communis*), lavender (*Lavandula dentata*), and scented geraniums (*Pelargonium* spp.) are all great choices for your first standards.

After selecting your plant, gather your supplies, starting with a container. I prefer clay pots over plastic. As the head of the topiary develops, the weight is at the top of the plant. A clay pot stabilizes your plant, keeping it from tipping over. You will also need bypass pruning shears, scissors, a stake to match the mature height of your plant, something for tying the plant to the stake, and potting soil. For herbs, I prefer a slightly barky soil mix—one that will hold moisture without becoming waterlogged or soggy. For rosemary and lavender, I add a heaping teaspoon of granulated dolomitic lime for each gallon of soil.

STAKE YOUR STEMS

The most critical part of creating a standard is forming a strong, straight stem. Line up the stake next to the stem, and push it down into the soil to the bottom of the pot. During the growing period, I use twist ties to secure the stem to the stake every few inches. For display, I replace the ties with raffia or ribbons. If the stem is straight, wrap the twist ties around the stem and stake several times, without twisting them. This allows the ties to expand as the stem grows. If the stem is slightly bent, you may have to twist the tie to hold the stem in place until it "learns" its new form. Make the twist against the stake to avoid damaging the stem.

If you start with a small plant but want a tall topiary, pot up and stake in stages. It is difficult to water a small plant in a large pot properly, and a long stake may start to wobble or pull your plant sideways.

PRUNE WHEN YOUR PLANT NEARS ITS MATURE HEIGHT

Keep leaf texture in mind when deciding the ultimate height of your standard. You want the overall proportions to be balanced. Large-leaved plants like rose geranium generally look better at 3 or 4 feet tall. You have more flexibility with small-leaved plants such as rosemary, myrtle, lavender, or 'Lemon Crispum' geranium—they look nice from 1 to 5 feet in height.

I used to remove all foliage from the stem as soon as I could, but this stunted plant growth—there wasn't enough leaf surface to photosynthesize food for the plant. Now I wait to remove foliage until I start forming the head.

When the stem is within a few inches of the height you want your mature standard to be, pinch out the growing tip, leave the top sets of branches, and remove the remaining lower branches or leaves from the stem with bypass pruners. Also, trim the stake to an inch or two below the foliage to keep it from interfering with the even development of the head.

As the remaining branches develop, let them grow to about four nodes (the swollen

Standards: Step-by-Step

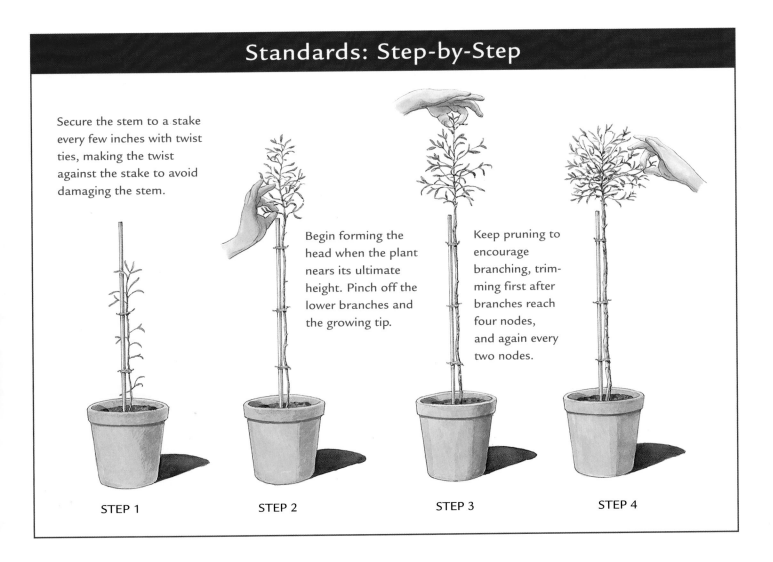

Secure the stem to a stake every few inches with twist ties, making the twist against the stake to avoid damaging the stem.

Begin forming the head when the plant nears its ultimate height. Pinch off the lower branches and the growing tip.

Keep pruning to encourage branching, trimming first after branches reach four nodes, and again every two nodes.

STEP 1 STEP 2 STEP 3 STEP 4

part of the branch that bears a leaf), then trim. You want a tight head with strong scaffolding, or inner branches. As the plant branches out, trim after every two nodes of growth. On plants with large branches, use bypass pruners to trim each branch individually. On fine-textured plants, you'll find that scissors give a smoother line.

GROW A STANDARD IN A YEAR

Standards put on their strongest growth in spring and summer. If you start in fall with a 4-inch pot of myrtle or rosemary, you should be able to finish a 2-foot standard in one year. A small plant started in spring will take about 18 months to mature because you'll be forming the head in winter when light levels

are low and growth has slowed. If you can find a healthy, gallon-sized plant in late winter or early spring, you may be able to finish the topiary by Christmas.

Water, fertilizer, plenty of light, and good air circulation are essential for maintaining healthy standards. However, overwatering and overfertilizing will force soft, weak growth. And while it's all right to occasionally hose off the foliage, do not mist rosemaries, as they are susceptible to fungus and disease.

If you are going to move plants inside to a sunny window for winter and out for summer, let them acclimate to their new conditions gradually. Plunking them down in the full sun when it warms up in spring can cause sunburn and leaf drop.

Potting *a* Japanese Maple

NANCY FIERS

and her husband, Don, own Mountain Maples, a Japanese-maple specialty nursery atop a mountain in Laytonville, California.

The diminutive leaves and carefully pruned branches of a Japanese maple complement a weathered redwood container.

BONSAI, OR GROWING TREES in a container, is an art, a science and a meditative practice. But the amount of time and dedication required to grow tiny trees in tiny pots is too great for many of us. More compatible to our lifestyle is growing dwarf trees in larger containers. They don't require such exacting care, and we can learn from bonsai horticultural techniques how to keep these beautiful trees healthy so that they grace our lives for many years. Watering and fertilizing regularly, along with pruning the roots and canopy every few years is all the attention most dwarf trees take.

There are many dwarf trees that can be grown in containers, but one of my favorites is the dwarf Japanese maple. Its fine texture and small size make it the perfect tree to use as the transition from indoor space to outdoor space, or to indicate the beginning of a path. A maple that is properly pruned can guide the eye toward your

doorway, or away from the house toward a beautiful view.

CHOOSE A WIDE POT

There are almost as many containers on the market as there are varieties of trees to plant in them. A container can enhance the beauty and significance of a tree, the way a frame enhances a painting. Choosing a container is mostly a matter of personal preference, but let me pass on a couple of my thoughts. Containers that are wider than they are tall are far more stable than tall, narrow ones. Also, wide containers have more space for ground covers, rocks, or other decorations.

Any container you choose should have several drainage holes in the bottom. Keep in mind that you can easily drill holes in a wood or plastic container; it might not be so easy in a ceramic one.

Wooden containers are attractive and affordable, and if they are made properly, they can last for many years. Beware of wood containers held together only by nails because, chances are, they'll fall apart very quickly. The redwood container used in these photographs has strong, interlocking box joints. A wood container with metal straps wrapping completely around it is also quite strong.

High-fired ceramic containers are a good choice because they won't break in a freeze, but large ceramic containers are very heavy. To tell whether a ceramic container is high-fired, moisten the bottom; if the pot absorbs any moisture, it is not high-fired. Most economical, perhaps, is a plastic pot, and attractive ones can be found.

A 15-gallon pot will comfortably hold a 4- or 5-foot tree, and a 30-gallon tub will support an 8-foot tree. Casters on the bottom of any type of large pot or tub will ease moving.

USE A SAND-BASED POTTING MIX

The soil used in container growing is very important, mainly because there is so little of it. The soil serves two main functions: It supports the tree, anchoring it into the pot, and it provides a medium for the delivery of nutrients, moisture, and air.

For Japanese maples, a sand-based soil is best. Sandy soils help develop the fine, fibrous roots necessary to sustain trees in pots, and sand is dense, adding weight and stability to the planting.

You can purchase a commercial potting mix with a high sand content, or you can make your own. Start with 1 part coarse sand, add 3 parts peat moss or ground bark to hold air and moisture, and 1 part compost to provide nutrients.

Raking out the roots removes old soil during repotting. Use a hand cultivator or similar tool to gently untangle the roots prior to potting.

SOONER OR LATER, YOU'LL HAVE TO ROOT-PRUNE

Before purchasing a tree, tip it out of its pot to make sure that it is not root-bound. The roots should be healthy and abundant. Look for roots that are fine and fibrous rather than large and woody. Only young fibrous root tips are able to take up water and nutrition. Large, woody roots that encircle the root ball waste valuable space needed for water, air and soil, and may choke the tree to death.

You may find a tree that is the perfect size and the perfect shape for the perfect container you've already bought. You tip the tree out of the pot at the nursery only to find a snarl of large, tough, old roots. A rule of thumb is that if the tree looks healthy, it probably is. If you buy the tree, you face the task of root-pruning.

Root-pruning is not really difficult, and it's essential to the long-term health of a potted tree. Even if the roots of your new tree don't

Large, woody roots don't absorb nutrients, and they take up valuable space in the container. Only the smaller fibrous roots absorb nutrients. Large roots should be pruned.

Next, finesse your hand pruners inside the root ball, and prune out any large, woody roots. At the same time, shorten up all of the roots, and remove any dead ones. This will encourage growth of vigorous, young feeder roots that will supply the tree with a maximum amount of food and water.

On some old trees that have been in a container for many years, you may find a compacted fibrous root ball without large encircling roots. In such cases, it may be hard to untangle the roots. It may be easiest to use a saw to cut off the bottom inch or two of the root ball and a knife to make vertical cuts in their fibrous mass.

TEASE SOIL AROUND THE ROOTS, THEN WATER

To repot the tree, place fresh potting mix in the bottom of the container, spread the tree's roots over the top, and then tease soil in

Create a miniature landscape with rocks, bulbs, and perennials. Prune so that tree is open and airy.

need root-pruning right away, it should be done every two to five years to keep any containerized Japanese maple healthy.

Gently comb out and untangle the roots, using a cultivator or a similar tool. Use your fingers—bonsai artists use chopsticks—to remove the old soil from the outside perimeter.

Shouldering is the process of removing soil from the top of the root ball—what would be the shoulders if the tree's trunk were its neck. Do not remove roots in this area, just the soil. Removing compacted soil from the top of the root ball encourages new root growth.

Shouldering encourages new root growth. Remove the soil from around the roots in the shaded area, shown above.

around the roots, gently firming the soil as you fill the pot.

The first watering will settle your maple into its new home. I like to immerse the whole container, up to the soil line, in a tub of water. This assures a thorough settling of the soil around the roots. If this is not possible, a patient top watering works well. Gently run enough water through so that it runs out the bottom of the container. Keep watering for several minutes more.

A LITTLE FERTILIZER GOES A LONG WAY

When you fertilize your Japanese maple, remember that the goal is to keep the tree healthy, happy, and growing slowly. You do not want to encourage rapid growth. You are growing a small, delicate tree in a container, not starting a lumber business.

So use nitrogen fertilizers in limited amounts except in spring, when you can apply more because the tree needs to produce a lot of leaves quickly. For container-grown Japanese maples, fish emulsion is the perfect fertilizer. It's a complete food, it's low in nitrogen, and it's easy to use.

A balanced fertilizer with micronutrients, formulated as slow-release granules and applied as a topdressing, is also good. Apply slow-release formulas early in the season, ideally as buds begin to swell. If you apply them in fall, they may promote tender new growth that can be damaged by frost.

PRUNE BIG BRANCHES WHEN TREES ARE DORMANT

Pruning the canopy of your container tree to remove crossing branches and excess growth should be done during very late winter to early spring, as buds begin to swell. If you are potting or repotting the tree at the same

Acute-angled leaders are a weak part of a tree's structure, and they should be removed. Pruning a young tree can dramatically change its shape.

time, pot first and prune second. When you begin with a very young tree, you have the opportunity of correcting any structural flaws such as weak, acute crotch angles and double, equal-size leaders.

Begin by studying the tree carefully. This may be the most important step in pruning. All cuts should follow the "coarse-to-fine" rule, which says that the main trunk is the most bold, or coarse, line; as you move away from the trunk of the tree, the lines should become finer.

Coarse branches high up in the tree should be removed, since they throw the form of the tree out of balance. The finished tree should be open, airy and welcoming, not dark and bulky.

Although major pruning always takes place during dormancy, you can do really fine pruning work in spring after the appearance of the second set of new leaves. Pinch off the growing tip on the branches you wish to become more complex, and remove all branchlets that grow straight up or down.

Group succulent plants to accentuate their intriguing textures. Terra-cotta bowls of *Echeveria* make a stunning collection for a patio or entryway.

DEAN KELCH

is a botanist and horticulturist pursuing plant research at the University of California. He serves on the board of the San Francisco Succulent and Cactus Society.

Growing
Succulents
Successfully
in Pots

Easy-to-Grow Succulents

Aeonium arboreum 'Schwarzkopf'
   (black tree houseleek)

Aloe brevifolia (short-leaf aloe)

Crassula ovata cvs. (jade plant)

Echeveria agavoides

Euphorbia milii (crown of thorns)

Euphorbia obesa (living baseball)

Faucaria tigrina (tiger jaws)

Gasteria liliputana

Graptopetalum paraguayense (ghost plant)

Haworthia retusa

Oreocereus celsianus (old man cactus)

Pleiospilos bolusii (mimicry plant)

Pleiospilos nelii (split rock)

Rebutia aureiflora

Sedum morganianum (burro's tail)

I LOVE GROWING PLANTS in containers, but many potted plants demand constant watering in warm weather. Luckily, succulents—my favorite plant group—naturally grow in dry conditions and adapt well to the wide moisture swings encountered in containers. Not only are succulents adaptable to potted culture, but their sculptural qualities are displayed to great advantage when grown in pots.

SUCCULENT PLANTS ALL STORE WATER

There's often confusion about the differences between cacti and succulents. Cacti, which are members of the Cactaceae family, are just one type of succulent. Other succulents —jade plants, agaves, yuccas, ice plants, living stones, aloes, and haworthias—come from other plant families. They all store water in their stems, leaves, or roots.

1. When repotting succulents, first remove as much old soil as possible from the root ball. Use a pointed implement to avoid damaging the roots.

2. Cover the drainage hole with a piece of mesh screen or a small pot shard. This keeps the soil from leaking out.

3. Add soil mix to the pot and center the succulent. Tap the pot to settle the soil and add more mix, if needed.

4. Depending on the pot size, position succulents about ½ to 1½ inches below the rim. A topdressing of gravel adds a decorative look and keeps soil from splashing out.

Most succulents are too tender to stay outside year-round in most of the U.S., but growing them in containers lets us bring them indoors for the winter. A few hardy succulents, such as house leeks (*Sempervivum* spp.), prairie prickly-pear (*Opuntia humifusa*), and Adam's needle (*Yucca filamentosa*)—can be kept outdoors year-round, even in USDA Hardiness Zone 5.

GOOD DRAINAGE IS THE KEY

Succulents grow well in either ceramic or plastic containers, as long as the pots have one or more drainage holes. I avoid those decorative containers that compete with the plant for attention, opting instead for simple pots with nonshiny glazes. When repotting succulents, I use a container only slightly larger than the root ball. When there's a lot of extra soil holding water, succulent roots can easily rot.

A basic succulent potting mix contains a heavier component that provides nutrients and texture, and an amendment that enhances drainage and aeration. Good heavier ingredients include high-quality potting mix or loamy sand. Amendments include pumice, expanded shale, and perlite. Sand improves drainage but not aeration.

After trying many amendments, my top choice is horticultural pumice. Some gardeners grow fussy, rot-prone species of succulents in pure pumice. For most succulents, however, the amendment should comprise one third to one half of the mix. Persnickety species such as certain dry desert cacti prefer a mix low in organic matter, such as one-half loamy sand and one-half pumice.

REPOT SUCCULENTS WITH CARE

The best time to repot succulents is before or right when growth begins, which is usually in springtime. If the plant is tightly wedged in the pot, I invert the plant and rap the pot on the edge of my potting bench.

I repot every new plant I buy into my own mix, since my growing conditions differ from those of commercial growers. Old soil that clings to a succulent's roots can stay wetter or drier than the new soil. So when repotting, I remove as much of the old soil as possible from a root ball. I don't water a newly repotted succulent or expose it to bright sun for 5 to 10 days, as the roots need time to heal. Then I gradually increase the light level and begin watering. When I repot a dormant plant, I don't water at all until the growing season begins.

I water actively growing plants once or twice a week in hot weather. Many succulents, such as echeverias and aloes, should be watered all year, with less water given in winter. Others, such as cacti and agaves, should be kept cool and dry during the winter. Whether they're grown indoors or outside, place succulents where they'll get bright light and good air circulation.

Contrary to popular opinion, potted succulents appreciate regular feeding, since nutrients are washed out of pots by frequent watering. I often add a dash of blood meal, bonemeal, or kelp meal to my potting mix. In addition, I feed succulents a liquid fertilizer during the growing season. My succulents love fish emulsion. If you can stand the smell, it's a great organic fertilizer. When I'm using synthetic fertilizers, I find that weekly feeding at one fifth to one third the recommended strength is sufficient.

PLANT SUCCULENTS ALONE OR IN COMPATIBLE GROUPINGS

Given their striking forms, succulents usually look best when there's just one plant or type of plant in each pot. A potted agave or columnar cactus functions as a living sculpture, and a clump of echeverias looks wonderfully textural.

Nevertheless, you can create successful container plantings with groups of succulents. First, the species must be compatible. Cacti, which need a cool, dry winter rest, should not be combined with plants needing water or warmth all year. Also avoid planting rapid growers, such as some sedums, with less robust types. When I create mixed groupings, I use small, clumping types of succulents, such as sedums, haworthias, and echeverias. Whatever succulents you grow, their dramatic structure and intriguing colors can be enjoyed with a minimum of care.

S. ANDREW SCHULMAN

is a Seattle-based land-
scape designer, garden
writer, and photographer.
He lectures frequently
on rose gardening and
garden design.

Growing
Roses
in
Containers

Compact roses like
'The Fairy' stay in scale
with their containers
without the need for
heavy pruning.
Growing small cultivars
in containers prevents
them from being
overwhelmed by
neighboring plants.

HUNDREDS OF ROSES are crammed
into my small urban garden. And since
an elaborate deck prevents me from
expanding my borders to accommodate
new plants, enlarging the collection has
become a challenge. Luckily, the deck does offer the
opportunity for plenty of large decorative containers,
which I routinely fill with roses.

Through trial and error, I've discovered that the tricks
to growing roses successfully as container plants are to
choose those rose varieties best suited to container culture, to start with adequately sized containers, and most
important, to follow a few basic cultural principles.

SELECT COMPACT ROSES
FOR CONTAINERS

When choosing roses for containers, I look for naturally
compact varieties that will stay in scale with their con-

"Growing full-size roses and their companion plants together in containers is gardening at its most intensive."

tainers without much heavy pruning. I also prefer repeat bloomers to maximize seasonal interest. I've had success with compact Polyantha roses like 'Baby Faurax' and 'The Fairy', while continuously blooming China roses, including 'Ducher' and 'Mutabilis', worked just as well. Fragrance is a plus, too, since containers can bring shorter-growing roses closer to the nose.

Most of my favorite container roses, however, lack the vigor and full, bushy habit I usually prefer in garden roses. Consider 'Rose du Roi', a 19th-century Portland rose that figures in the pedigrees of most modern red roses. Despite its historical import, 'Rose du Roi' is

seldom planted, perhaps because its very low, open habit and slow growth make it awkward to place in the mixed border. Ironically, these same traits make 'Rose du Roi' an ideal container plant. The sparse, angular branches leave plenty of room for the plum and silver foliage of *Heuchera* 'Persian Carpet', which in turn provides a superb foil for the rose's large, flat, crimson flowers. Though even the larger-growing Portland roses like 'Rembrandt' and 'Marchesa Boccella' can make fine container plants, 'Rose du Roi' grows so slowly that it rarely outgrows its pot.

'Kronprincessin Viktoria', a sport of the famous Bourbon rose 'Souvenir de la Malmaison', has stunning white flowers of impressive fragrance, form, and size. But the plant itself has always struck me as weak and spindly, with stiff canes and a rigid habit. Certain that neighboring border plants would quickly overwhelm it, I tried 'Kronprincessin Viktoria' in a cast concrete container. To help flesh out the rose's sparse foliage, I paired it with *Hemerocallis* 'Frosted Pink Ice', known for slow growth and limited clump size. The two now cohabitate happily, with the deep purple foliage and magenta blooms of *Sedum* 'Vera Jameson' at their feet.

Since my garden grows on heavy clay that becomes waterlogged in winter, the rose containers are my only opportunity to grow such plants as *Sedum* species that demand open, well-drained soil. Rose-pink *Diascia* species that would expire in my borders after one wet Seattle winter thrive underneath the beautiful old cream and pink Tea rose 'Madame Antoine Mari'. *Sempervivum* species that would rot in the open ground multiply freely alongside the fragrant white China rose 'Ducher', while finicky Pacific Coast iris hybrids share space with the blush-pink Polyantha rose 'Clotilde Soupert'.

Some of the Best Roses for Pots

CULTIVAR	FLOWER COLOR	GROWTH HABIT*
'Baby Faurax'	amethyst	compact
'Clotilde Soupert'	pale pink	compact
'Ducher'	white	compact
'Hermosa'	pink	compact
'Kronprincessin Viktoria'	white	medium
'Lady Ann Kidwell'	deep pink	compact
'Madame Antoine Mari'	cream and pink	medium
'Marchesa Boccella'	light pink	medium
'Marie Pavié'	white	compact
'Mutabilis'	yellow changing to pink	medium
'Rembrandt'	brick-red	medium
'Rose du Roi'	crimson	compact
'The Fairy'	light pink	compact

*Compact cultivars generally grow no larger than 3 feet tall and wide. Medium cultivars may grow up to 4 feet tall and wide.

USE APPROPRIATE CONTAINERS AND POTTING MIX

Growing full-size roses and their companion plants together in containers is gardening at its most intensive. An adequately sized container and a few special cultural measures are crucial for success. The smallest container I'll consider for a rose is 20 inches across, and 24- to 36-inch-wide containers are my ideal. For durability, I lean toward cast stone or molded resin. While the popular half whisky barrels are a good size, they tend to decompose in my climate unless heavily treated with preservatives.

No matter what the material, proper drainage is essential. If the containers I choose lack drainage holes, I perforate their bottoms in several places with a power drill fitted with a ½-inch bit.

The choice of potting soil is also important in maintaining healthy growth. I use a commercial potting mix that includes a high percentage of organic matter, along with plenty of perlite and sharp sand to enhance drainage and air volume. To keep my container roses growing happily, I repot them every three or four years into fresh potting soil. I do this toward the end of winter dormancy, pruning the canes hard and rinsing all of the old soil off the plant's roots. If a plant is root-bound, I put it into a larger container and carefully prune away any roots that encircled the old pot. Repotting also gives me the opportunity to divide and move the various perennial companion plants in each container.

REMEMBER TO WATER AND FERTILIZE

Container-grown roses are liable to dry out quickly and require frequent watering. I check my containers for water nearly every day during the spring and summer, even if

the weather has been rainy. In my experience, natural rainfall is rarely, if ever, sufficient to sustain a rose in a container. Even with automated irrigation, it is wise to check the soil frequently for water, since uptake and evaporation vary considerably during the season.

With such frequent watering, nutrients tend to leach from the soil very rapidly. To counteract this loss, I apply a dilute, complete, water-soluble fertilizer to my container roses once a week. I begin feeding when

Half whisky barrels are the perfect size for compact roses like 'Hermosa'. You may need to treat the barrels with a water-based preservative to prevent the wood from decomposing.

Grow roses in durable containers made from cast stone or molded resin. This 'Marchesa Boccella' is growing in a cast-concrete urn.

growth emerges in the early spring and cut back in September so the summer growth has time to harden off before the first winter frosts. To supplement the organic content of the soil, I topdress each container generously with organic compost in autumn. Be sure to avoid overfeeding container-grown roses with high-nitrogen fertilizers. Too much nitrogen will cause excessive leaf growth at the expense of bloom while encouraging your roses to outgrow their containers.

BRING ROSES INSIDE FOR THE WINTER

Roses in containers are a bit more vulnerable to cold than they would be in the open ground. Even here in USDA Zone 8, I coddle my more tender Tea roses by wrapping their containers in a layer of home insulation secured with heavy plastic. I've even lugged some of my most delicate container-grown roses into covered shelter at the threat of a sudden early freeze. Of course, by planting in lightweight containers set on wheeled bases, cold-climate gardeners can grow even the most tender Tea and China roses. Simply move the containers into shelter at winter's onset.

I won't deny that growing old garden roses and shrub roses in containers entails a bit of fuss. But gardeners willing to make the effort may find, as I have, that container gardening offers exciting opportunities for planting design, and a chance to grow roses they might not otherwise be able to.

MARK KANE

is a former editor of *Fine Gardening* and currently serves as the garden editor of *Better Homes and Gardens*. He lives in Des Moines, Iowa, gardening in prairie soil.

Forcing Bulbs

Tulips are among the many spring-flowering bulbs ideally suited to forcing. They require four to five months of chilling, but will flower two or three weeks.

L AST DECEMBER, MY HOUSE had an early spring. While snow fell outside, the long bay window in the dining room bloomed with spring flowers. Grape hyacinths raised their blue spikes; daffodils assembled in white and yellow drifts; tiny miniature irises with blue petals and yellow throats crowded together in 4-inch pots. When I came downstairs in the morning, the welcome smell of flowers met my nose and the sight of sunlit colors made the start of the gardening year seem just a little bit closer.

I owed my wintertime harvest of color and fragrance to forcing, an old trick that fools bulbs into blooming early. Forcing is an easy thing to do. You will need potting mix, pots, and a spot that will stay reliably cold but not freezing, from late fall onward. And you need some hardy, spring-flowering bulbs, such as crocuses, hyacinths, scillas, tulips, and daffodils. But before I tell you how to force bulbs, let me explain why forcing works.

WHAT HAPPENS WHEN YOU FORCE BULBS

The bulbs that are suited to forcing have a topsy-turvy cycle of growth in nature and in the garden. Most of them flower early in spring while trees are still bare. Their leaves and roots persist just long enough—through mid to late spring—for the bulbs to store a new supply of energy. Then the leaves and roots die and the bulbs, safe underground, go dormant for the summer and part of the fall.

In fall, when the soil cools, the bulbs awaken and send out new roots, the first step in their preparation for the next spring. The roots continue to grow until the soil cools to 40° F. In most of the U.S., the bulbs produce a dense mat of roots before winter sets in. In cold climates, freezing temperatures halt the roots' growth, but they won't kill them; in warmer climates, the bulbs may keep making roots throughout the whole winter.

When spring temperatures rise into the 40s and 50s, bulbs reawaken, send up leaves, then make flowers. This growth is rapid, thanks to the full complement of roots, so leaves have plenty of time before they decline to replenish the energy of the bulbs. Then the bulbs go dormant again until fall.

Forcing exploits this cycle. In fall, you buy dormant bulbs, pot them and keep them cold for several months to stimulate them to make roots. Once plants have roots, you bring the pots to a windowsill, where the warmth persuades the bulbs that spring has arrived. In short order, they flower, and you have an early spring.

HOW TO START FORCING BULBS

The first step in forcing is to buy bulbs in fall, about six weeks before hard freezes are due. In much of the U.S., the right time comes sometime in September. Garden centers offer a selection then that includes the mainstays of the spring garden. Look for bulbs that are firm, free of mold, and uniform in size. From mail-order specialists you can order not only the mainstays, but also lesser-known bulbs. Prices are modest—about 10 cents to 50 cents a bulb.

Next, gather up pots in which to plant your bulbs. Almost any pot will do, provided there's enough room for roots. Pots with drainage holes and saucers are safest because they make it hard to drown roots. You can also use pots with no drainage holes, but you

A Parade of Bulbs

Bulbs for forcing vary in shape and size.
Shoots grow from the top; roots from the bottom.
Plant bottom-end-down.

Emerging new shoot

Top

Daffodil   Puschkinia   Grape hyacinth   Dwarf iris   Crocus   Glory of the snow

must water these pots with a light hand to avoid a lake in the bottom.

Use ordinary potting mix. It provides air spaces and a considerable capacity to retain moisture. You can buy it ready-made or mix your own. My recipe is 1 part shredded peat moss and 1 part perlite (small, light beads of volcanic glass). For top-heavy bulbs like daffodils (*Narcissus* spp.) planted in light plastic containers, add ¼ part sand; the extra weight helps anchor the containers.

When you plant the bulbs, put them high in the pot and space them closely. Fill a pot ¾ full with potting mix. Set the bulbs close together on top of the mix, and then add more mix to cover them. Most bulbs for forcing are so small—under ¾ inch in diameter—that you can space them less than 1 inch apart. Close spacing looks good. A dozen grape hyacinths (*Muscari* spp.) in a 6-inch pot make a strong show of color, and the crowding doesn't bother them. The exceptions are daffodils and paperwhites (*Narcissus tazetta*); both need about 1 to 2 inches of space between bulbs.

I like to grow small bulbs such as crocuses (*Crocus vernus* and *C. chrysanthus*) or grape hyacinths in 4-inch pots. Then I can gather five or six pots at a time on the windowsill in

Scilla

Bulbs and Times for Forcing

Here are 17 bulbs that can be forced for winter bloom:

NAME	WEEKS OF COLD	WEEKS OF BLOOM
Crocus (*Crocus chrysanthus*)	15	2-3
Dutch crocus (*Crocus vernus*)	15	2
Daffodils (*Narcissus* spp.)	15-17	2-3
Checkered lily (*Fritillaria meleagris*)	15	3
Glory of the snow (*Chionodoxa luciliae*)	15	2-3
Grape hyacinth (*Muscari armeniacum*)	13-15	2-3
Grape hyacinth (*Muscari botryoides f. album*)	14-15	2-3
Hyacinth (*Hyacinthus* spp.)	11-14	2-3
Iris (*Iris danfordiae*)	15	2-3
Iris (*Iris reticulata*)	15	2-3
Paperwhites (*Narcissus tazetta*)	none	3-5
Striped squill (*Puschkinia scilloides* var. *libanotia*)	15	2-3
Siberian squill (*Scilla siberica*)	15	2-3
Scilla (*Scilla mischtschenkoana*)	12-15	2-3
Common snowdrop (*Galanthus nivalis*)	15	2
Tulip (*Tulipa* spp.)	14-20	2-3
Winter aconite (*Eranthis hyemalis*)	15	2

any combination I please—all grape hyacinths to make a single sweep of color or a mix of bulbs for variety. You can get the same effects in larger pots by planting them full with one kind of bulb or by mixing several kinds together. It's tricky to mix bulbs because they may flower at different times, but you might as well experiment—you'll still have flowers, and you'll learn what works.

THE RIGHT KIND OF COLD

Once you pot your bulbs, you have to keep them cold and moist. They need three or more months of cold, dark, humid conditions to make roots. (Paperwhites are exceptions. They don't require chilling and are

How to Force Bulbs

INTO THE POT To force bulbs for winter bloom, start in fall by setting dormant bulbs, with the root end down and shoot end up, into a container three-quarters full of potting mix. The bulbs shown here are grape hyacinths.

CLOSE SPACING Seven bulbs fill a pot that's 6 inches in diameter. Close spacing yields a dramatic show of flowers. Potting mix partially covers the bulbs in the second pot, making it ready for chilling.

ready to grow and flower as soon as you pot them and set them on the windowsill.)

The simplest way to chill bulbs is to store them in your refrigerator. The temperature on the shelves is about 40°F, suitable for root growth, but refrigerators are as dry as deserts, so water the pots well, put them in plastic bags, and tie the tops of the bags to keep the mix moist. Check the pots once a month and water as needed.

> *"I owed my wintertime harvest of color and fragrance to forcing, an old trick that fools bulbs into blooming early."*

If you don't want to use up your refrigerator space with pots of bulbs, there are other methods of chilling. Bulbs can be carefully buried in dry straw or leaves outdoors, placed into a cold frame, or stored on cellar stairs.

If you want to insulate your bulbs with leaves, first, pot them. Then gather up a supply of dry leaves and heap them up into a fluffy pile with plenty of air spaces. Next, choose a sheltered spot, safe from the northerly winds of winter—against your house, in the corner between your garage and compost pile, or next to a board fence, perhaps. Arrange your containers there in a tight circle. You can stack a second, smaller circle on top of the first. Now rake up your dry leaves and heap them 1 foot deep over the containers. Spread them at least 1 foot

WATERING TRICK While bulbs are chilling, they need moist potting mix in which to make good roots. Enclosing a watered pot in a plastic bag will keep the mix moist for a month or more. In the cold, the bulbs make roots, preparing themselves for spring and the return of warmth when they will make leaves and flowers.

READY TO GO Removed from the pot, a group of grape hyacinths knits the potting mix together with plump white roots. When roots poke out the drainage hole and fill the pot, bulbs are ready to move into the light, where the pale shoots will quickly turn dark green.

beyond the circle of containers, then lightly drape a sheet of plastic or a tarp over the pile of leaves to keep them dry, and anchor the edges with bricks, stones, or 2x4s. Insulated by the leaves, your containers will stay cold but not frozen. To check their progress, just lift one edge of the tarp, reach through the leaves and pull out a container.

You can also chill your containers in a cold frame, but only if you're sure the cold frame stays cold. On a sunny day in early winter, even if the outside temperature is well below freezing, a cold frame can heat up to 60°F or 70°F. This heat could prompt the bulbs to start making leaves and flowers. Keep the temperature inside the cold frame low by opening the top in the morning; close it again

in the late afternoon to keep temperatures from dropping below freezing. And be sure to water the pots when they need it.

If your basement has a set of outside stairs with a storm cover, you can also chill bulbs there. Late last fall, I set 48 pots of bulbs, closed inside plastic garbage bags, on the landing at the foot of my basement stairs, a spot that's about 4 feet underground. For the next three months, the temperature there ranged from near-freezing to about 45°F— ideal for growing roots and chilling bulbs. Heat from the earth surrounded the containers; cold air poured down the stairs from the loose-fitting storm cover, but it was buffered by air in the 60s just 1 foot away on the other side of the basement door.

A gallery of forced spring bulbs paints a windowsill with color. The brown bells of fritillary bloom in the foreground; behind them are daffodils (LEFT) and a pot of tulips with a skirt of golden crocuses (RIGHT).

"When I came downstairs in the morning, the welcome smell of flowers met my nose and the sight of sunlit colors made the start of the gardening year seem just a little bit closer."

HERE COME THE FLOWERS

When your bulbs have chilled for about three months, start checking their progress as indicated by root growth. Don't be misled into thinking they're ready to take out of the cold by a shoot poking up through the potting mix. To be sure about the bulbs, lift each pot and look at the bottom. If you see plump, white roots poking through the drainage holes, the bulbs are ready to come out of the cold.

The timing varies from one kind of bulb to another; some bulbs need just three months of chilling while others require four months, and some tulips may need five months. You can always put pots that already have good roots back into the cold for a few more weeks.

When your bulbs are ready, bring them to a bright windowsill or sunroom. They need the light so their leaves and flower stems will grow short and sturdy—in weak light they'd produce tall and lanky flower stems that are likely to flop over.

Water the pots with care. Before leaves appear, you may have to water only every second or third day. Once leaves appear, you may have to water every day. In both cases, wait until the surface of the potting mix is dry to the touch. If you want to keep the bulbs growing until spring so you can plant them in the garden as perennials, give them a weak solution of fertilizer from time to time.

Forcing does seem to shorten the bloom time of most bulbs. For example, indoors, grape hyacinths remain fragrant and presentable for about a week. Outdoors, they last two to three weeks. I think the difference has to do with temperature. Outdoors, in early spring, cool days and cold nights slow the onset of maturity. Indoor temperatures, however, stay close to 70°F both day and night, hastening the flowers' maturity and decline. To accommodate shortened bloom periods, force a lot of bulbs and bring only a few at a time to the windowsill. By staggering their bloom, you'll have plenty of bulbs either in flower or awaiting their turn in the cold. Your spring can begin as early as December and last until the outdoor trees leaf out.

Credits

The articles compiled in this book appeared in the following issues of *Fine Gardening*:

p. 6: Pots Have a Place in the Garden (originally With or Without Plants, Pots Have a Place in the Garden) by Gordon Hayward, issue 56. Photos © Stephen Swinburne.

p. 10: A Movable Garden by Sydney Eddison, issue 69. Photos by Steve Silk, © The Taunton Press, Inc.

p. 18: A Tiny Water Garden (originally Make a Big Splash with a Tiny Water Garden) by Joseph Tomocik, issue 56. Photos by Steve Silk, © The Taunton Press, Inc.

p. 26: A Penthouse Garden by Keith Corlett, issue 11. Photos on p. 26 by Susan Kahn, © The Taunton Press, Inc.; pp. 29 and 31 by staff.

p. 32: The Art of Container Gardening by Michael Bowell, issue 24. Photos on pp. 32, 35, and 36 by staff; p. 33 (author photo) by Judy Glanville.

p. 38: Potted Plantings in the Shade (originally Grow Spectacular Potted Plantings in the Shade) by Gary Keim, issue 71. Photos by Lee Anne White, © The Taunton Press, Inc.

p. 44: Creative Plant Combinations by Sydney Eddison, issue 57. Photos on pp. 44, 46, 47 © Lee Anne White; p. 45 (author photo) by Steve Silk, © The Taunton Press, Inc.

p. 48: Planting for All-Season Interest (originally Planting Containers for All-Season Interest) by B. B. Stamats, issue 65. Photos on p. 48 © B. B. Stamats; p. 49 (author photo) by David Barnhizer; p. 50 © J. Paul Moore (garden of Tara Dillard, Stone Mountain, GA).

p. 52: Pair Plants for Eye-Catching Containers (originally Pair Striking Plants for Eye-Catching Container Gardens) by June Hutson, issue 60. Photos © Amy Ziffer.

p. 56: Window Boxes to Suit the Season by Gary Keim, issue 42. Photos on pp. 56, 58, 60, and 62 by Delilah Smittle, © The Taunton Press, Inc.; p. 63 © Susan Kahn. Illustrations by Vince Babak.

p. 64: Focus on Foliage for a Soothing Setting by Lee Anne White, issue 75. Photos © Lee Anne White.

p. 70: Three-Season Container Plantings by Wesley Rouse, issue 37. Photos on p. 70 © Lee Anne White; pp. 71–75 and 77 by Chris Curless, © The Taunton Press, Inc.

p. 80: Lots of Pots by Melissa McLaughlin, issue 55 (includes a sidebar from A Pot for Any Plant by Delilah Smittle, issue 36). Photos on pp. 80 and 82 © Lee Anne White; pp. 83 and 84 by Scott Phillips, © The Taunton Press, Inc.; p. 85 © Susan Kahn.

p. 86: New Life for Old Housewares (originally Give New Life to Old Housewares) by J-P Malocsay, issue 70. Photos © J-P Malocsay.

p. 91: A Hoop Trellis for Containers (originally A Hoop Trellis Adds an English Accent) by Kate Hunter, issue 55. Photos on p. 91 (top) by Rachel Hunter; pp. 91 (bottom), 92, 94, and 95 by Steve Silk, © The Taunton Press, Inc. Illustration by Christine Erikson.

p. 96: Build a Classic Planter Box by Mario Rodriguez, issue 66. Photos on p. 96 by Lee Anne White, © The Taunton Press, Inc.; p. 97 (author photo) by Anatole Burkin; p. 99 by Vincent Laurence, © The Taunton Press, Inc. Illustration by Mark Sant'Angelo.

p. 101: Create an Elegant Hanging Basket by Heather McCain, issue 61. Photos by Virginia Small, © The Taunton Press, Inc.

p. 108: Evaluating Potting Soil by Rita Buchanan, issue 12. Photos on pp. 108, 110–112, and 116 by Susan Kahn, © The Taunton Press, Inc.; p. 109 (author photo) by Steve Buchanan.

p. 118: Drip Irrigation Makes Watering a Cinch by Steve Silk, issue 73. Photos by Virginia Small, © The Taunton Press, Inc.

p. 124: A Simple Guide to Repotting Plants by James Kramer, issue 77. Photos by Jodie Delohery, © The Taunton Press, Inc.

p. 129: Tending Tender Plants in Winter by Sydney Eddison, issue 63. Photos on 129, 130, 132 by Steve Silk, © The Taunton Press, Inc.; pp. 131, 133 © Lee Anne White.

p. 136: Summer-Flowering Bulbs by Rob Proctor, issue 36. Photos on pp. 136, 138 by Rob Proctor, courtesy Simon and Schuster; p. 140 (top) by Chris Curless, © The Taunton Press, Inc.; p. 140 (middle and bottom) © David Cavagnaro; p. 141 by Rob Proctor.

p. 142: Grow Your Own Herb Standard by Denise Smith, issue 59. Photos on p. 142 © Lee Anne White; p.143 by Lee Anne White, © The Taunton Press, Inc. Illustration by Gary Williamson.

p. 146: Potting a Japanese Maple by Nancy Fiers, issue 50. Photos on p. 147 © Amy Ziffer; pp. 148–151 by Charles Kennard, © The Taunton Press, Inc. Illustrations by Sharon D. Siegel.

p. 152: Growing Succulents Successfully in Pots by Dean Kelch, issue 69. Photos by Lee Anne White, © The Taunton Press, Inc.

p. 156: Growing Roses in Containers (originally Growing Garden Roses in Containers) by S. Andrew Schulman, issue 78. Photos on pp. 156, 159, 160 © J. Paul Moore; p. 157 (author photo) by S. Andrew Schulman.

p. 161: Forcing Bulbs by Mark Kane, issue 34. Photos on p. 161 courtesy Heath Enterprises; pp. 162 and 164–165 by Susan Kahn, © The Taunton Press, Inc.; p. 166 courtesy International Bloembollen Centrum.

Front matter photo credits

p. ii: Steve Silk, © The Taunton Press, Inc.
p. iv: © J. Paul Moore.
Contents (from left): Steve Silk, © The Taunton Press, Inc.; © Lee Anne White; © J-P Malocsay; Jodie Delohery, © The Taunton Press, Inc. (top); © David Cavagnaro (bottom).
p. 2: Chris Curless, © The Taunton Press, Inc.

Section openers photo credits

pp. 4–5: Steve Silk, © The Taunton Press, Inc.
p. 42: © Amy Ziffer.
p. 43: © Lee Anne White.
p. 78: J-P Malocsay.
p. 79: Steve Silk, © The Taunton Press, Inc.
p. 106: Susan Kahn, © The Taunton Press, Inc.
p. 107: Jodie Delohery, © The Taunton Press, Inc.
p. 134: Lee Anne White, © The Taunton Press, Inc.
p. 135: Rob Proctor, courtesy Simon and Schuster.

Index